Think LIKE A STRIPPER

Business Lessons to Up Your Confidence,
Attract More Clients & Rule Your Market

ERIKA LYREMARK

BASCOM HILL PUBLISHING GROUP

Bascom Hill Publishing Group
212 3rd Avenue North, Suite 290
Minneapolis, MN 55401
612.455.2293
www.bascomhillbooks.com

ISBN-13: 978-1-62652-113-1
LCCN: 2013905701

Distributed by Itasca Books

Book Design by Kristeen Ott
Moments Shared Photography
Makeup by Nicole Fae

Printed in the United States of America

BASCOM HILL
PUBLISHING GROUP

If instead of fulfilling your business potential
and happy-dancing in your stilettos,
you're crying in the bathroom and
wrecking your mascara,
then this book is dedicated to you.

For Chad Haverfield, my friend and comrade,
who passed away unexpectedly in August 2010.
Chad helped make this book come alive,
providing guidance, encouragement, ideas and words.

Chad, I miss you terribly. Thank you so much for
letting me borrow your angel writing wings
and helping me believe that I could do this.

Introduction: Wisdom from the Strip / xiii

1. Wake Up. Game On! / 1
Stripper Tip #1: *Always Have a Red Carpet Dream / 1*
Stripper Tip #2: *Count the Pros, Not the Cons / 4*
Stripper Tip #3: *Create a Stage Name / 6*
Stripper Tip #4: *Don't Work the Low End of the Stripper Pole / 9*
Stripper Tip #5: *Big Girls Take Baby Steps / 10*
Stripper Tip #6: *You're Already Naked, So Go for It / 12*
Stripper Tip #7: *Put On Your Training Heels / 14*
Stripper Tip #8: *Remove the Safety Net / 15*
Stripper Tip #9: *Serve. Don't Sell. / 16*
Stripper Tip #10: *Shake It 'Til You Make It / 18*

2. Sell It, Baby! / 21
Stripper Tip #11: *Know Your Business Seductress Style / 21*
Stripper Tip #12: *Strap On Your Blinders / 23*
Stripper Tip #13: *Put On Your Big-Girl Panties / 25*
Stripper Tip #14: *Walk In As If You Have the Job / 27*
Stripper Tip #15: *Ask for the Dance / 29*
Stripper Tip #16: *"Maybe Later" Means "No" / 30*
Stripper Tip #17: *It Takes Tricks to Turn "Tricks" / 32*
Stripper Tip #18: *Pump Yourself Up to Pimp Yourself Out / 34*
Stripper Tip #19: *Be Your Own Best Playmate / 35*
Stripper Tip #20: *Get a Comrade of Kick-Ass / 37*
Stripper Tip #21: *Catch More Business with Honey / 39*
Stripper Tip #22: *Get Back On the Pole / 40*

3. Make Them Want You! / 43

Stripper Tip #23: *You Are the Muscle in Your Hustle / 43*

Stripper Tip #24: *Free Samples Get 'Em in the Door / 45*

Stripper Tip #25: *You Only Need Two Bikinis / 47*

Stripper Tip #26: *Always Be Seducing / 49*

Stripper Tip #27: *Be Queen of Your Domain / 50*

Stripper Tip #28: *Turn Your Customers On / 52*

Stripper Tip #29: *Define "Stupid" / 54*

Stripper Tip #30: *Let Your Brand Hustle for You / 55*

4. Strip Smart! / 59

Stripper Tip #31: *Invest Your Tips / 59*

Stripper Tip #32: *Adopt a Stripper's Business Plan / 61*

Stripper Tip #33: *Resist the Sweetness of a Sugar Daddy / 63*

Stripper Tip #34: *Business Before Pleasure / 64*

Stripper Tip #35: *Bring Your B-Cup Game / 66*

Stripper Tip #36: *Upgrade to Double-Ds / 67*

Stripper Tip #37: *Think Outside the Candy Box / 69*

Stripper Tip #38: *Be Blonde for a Buck / 71*

Stripper Tip #39: *Following the Rules Won't Make You Rich / 72*

Stripper Tip #40: *Communicate About the Cash / 74*

Stripper Tip #41: *Know When to Leave Las Vegas / 76*

5. Keep It Simple, Sexy! / 79

Stripper Tip #42: *Crack Your Own Whip / 79*

Stripper Tip #43: *Work Like the Rent Is Due / 81*

Stripper Tip #44: *Don't Light Your Own Cigarette / 82*

Stripper Tip #45: *Give It Your Least / 84*

Stripper Tip #46: *Level Up (And Let Them Adjust!) / 86*

Stripper Tip #47: *Take a Break from Heelsville / 87*

Stripper Tip #48: *Know When to End the Dance* / 89
Stripper Tip #49: *Take a Chore Break* / 90
Stripper Tip #50: *It's Okay to Put On Your One-Inch Stilettos* / 92
Stripper Tip #51: *Become a Mistress of Patience* / 94

6. Be On Top! / 97
Stripper Tip #52: *Give Your Self-Confidence a Massage* / 97
Stripper Tip #53: *Be Aggressively Positive* / 99
Stripper Tip #54: *Practice Radical Gratitude* / 101
Stripper Tip #55: *It's All Part of the Act* / 103
Stripper Tip #56: *Tune Them Out, Tune You In* / 104
Stripper Tip #57: *Nice Girls Say No* / 106
Stripper Tip #58: *Refuse to Be Bullied* / 108
Stripper Tip #59: *B-Slap Your Obstacles Down* / 110

7. Don't Be That Girl! / 113
Stripper Tip #60: *Avoid the Unemployment Couch* / 113
Stripper Tip #61: *Don't Let the Throw Rug Distract You* / 115
Stripper Tip #62: *Never Gossip About Your Competition* / 117
Stripper Tip #63: *Don't Forget Where You Came From* / 118
Stripper Tip #64: *Never Complain in the Company of Customers* / 120
Stripper Tip #65: *Don't Strip Off the Clock* / 121
Stripper Tip #66: *Don't Dance for Difficult People* / 123
Stripper Tip #67: *Jealousy Kills—It Doesn't Pay the Bills!* / 124
Stripper Tip #68: *You Are a Princess. Take Charge.* / 126

Your Next Dance Moves / 129
Strip-O-Pedia / 131
Radical Gratitude / 133
About the Author / 135

INTRODUCTION

Wisdom from the Strip

While constructing this book, I ran into a problem. During the nine years I danced, there were two stories happening. There was the Erika who was ambitious and optimistic, who knew she was meant for great things—the Erika who loved school and dreamt of one day being a hugely successful businesswoman. Then there was the Erika who truly thought she could survive the enormity of the adult entertainment industry. I started out strong, naïve and believing in the freedom to express my sexuality and to exploit my body for profit. I was young, headstrong and, as it turned out, not as smart as I thought I was. The last five years I danced, I was depressed, anxious and hopeless. And by year seven, I was looking for happiness in a bottle.

Broken by the life I arrogantly thought I was superior to, in the end, I was blessed with assistance from friends, family and many other supporters who helped me exit the industry.

When I left the strip club world in 2001, the only people who knew that I used to be a stripper were my family, the few friends I had remained close with and my then-boyfriend—now my husband. I was self-conscious of the time I'd spent on the pole and saw no reason to bring it up. Ever.

However, life had a different plan for me. In 2005,

when I decided I wanted to have a global company, I knew
that I would have to tell my story, or someone else would.
But I didn't want to write the typical story that's usually
told. I didn't want it to be an autobiography of victimhood.
I wasn't a victim. I wasn't abused or forced into the industry.
I wanted to share the important business and life lessons I'd
learned while swinging around the pole. It took a lot of yoga,
meditation and coaching, but I was able to not only make
peace with my past but embrace it. With a bit of distance
between me and the pole, I was able to see the strength in my
history, not just the depression that I'd suffered because of it.

Being a stripper requires courage. Thousands of men—
and women—have seen me onstage, spinning and twirling in
my birthday suit. (Well, I did have shoes on.) I've performed
more lap dances than I can count for every type of person:
business executive, rock star, accountant, construction
worker, farmer, celebrity, professional athlete and college
student. I've worked in the same room as my cutthroat
competitors. I've seen dancers steal one another's clothes
and cash. One time, a dancer even punched another dancer
in the face with a drinking glass, sending her straight to the
emergency room. I've had to negotiate with disrespectful
strip club managers, cheesy DJs, macho bouncers, perverts
and jerks—all while working my way through my college
degrees in Apparel Design and in Women Studies. You
might not picture a girl in a G-string tackling a degree in
Women Studies, but I've got the transcript to prove it.

But it wasn't in the classroom and it wasn't through
my "respectable" career pursuits that I learned how to
succeed in business.

I learned it on the pole.

Every bit of success I have these days can be traced back to my trials and triumphs in the club. If I could survive nearly a decade bathed in neon and sweat and go on to co-create a multimillion-dollar commercial real estate company as well as launch Daily Whip, my business coaching company, I knew others could benefit from my story, too. I just didn't know how to tell it . . . until 2009, when I noticed an unsettling mood sweeping over my clients.

The shaky-economy doomsday gloom spewing from every media outlet was poisoning my clients' thoughts, and they were second-guessing their abilities to succeed. I remember watching a report on a morning talk show claiming that America wasn't in the throes of a financial crisis, but, rather, a *confidence* crisis. Investors feared their money wouldn't produce returns, and Americans were responding by hoarding cash instead of spending it. The same fear infiltrating the country seemed to be paralyzing my clients. I couldn't let that happen. I needed to find an inspiring way to convey my belief in them so that they could proceed in their businesses with confidence.

After having lunch with a colleague who was expressing concerns about his own business, I had an epiphany. I'd been in his situation before, so I told him a story that I thought would inspire him.

You see, it wasn't every night that the club was packed with customers ready to hand over their weekly pay. Some nights were slow. And on those nights, when customers were few and far between, every stripper became obsessed with finding the costume that would make her the most cash.

First, she'd try the polka-dot bikini. Then she'd put on the Hawaiian style bikini with palm trees and coconuts and head back out to see if it would make her more money. Then she'd don the ever-popular hot-pink bikini and see what the meager crowd thought of her in that one. If that didn't net her the results she craved, she might swing back to polka dots, or rummage through the dressing room for something new. It was the same with shoes: silver glitter platforms, metallic gold pumps, strappy white stilettos, black thigh-high leather boots. Hairstyles flew into a blur of up-dos, down-dos, ponytails and pigtails.

Imagine a never-ending stream of three dozen women flooding in and out of a cramped dressing room, frantically trying to find the outfit guaranteed to snag her another lap dance. It was mayhem! Chaos! And I was one of those desperate, crazy ladies.

On one of these slow nights, I was in an unusually good mood, even though I was certain I wouldn't be coming home with lots o' coin. I was tired of all the costume changes—and extra loads of laundry!—so I decided on that night, I wasn't going to give a hot damn about making money. I was simply going to have a good time. I didn't comb my hair, or fix my lipstick, or powder my nose, or refresh my perfume. I wore the same outfit all night long, and eventually I looked more like a mug shot than a showgirl. I spent the night laughing my ass off, asking for ridiculous amounts of money just to see if I could get it. And you know what? It was one of the best hustles of my life. Clearly, making money had less to do with my bikini than with my attitude.

I hadn't realized it before, but that strategy had stuck with me, and I had put it to work again and again. And that day at lunch, as I saw my colleague's eyes filling with hope about the economic possibilities of making "fun" a part of his business plan, I knew I had to share more of these stripper stories. So I blogged about it and named my post "It's Not About the Bikini: Nine Steps to Thrive in the New Economy." I knew that if my clients could embrace just this one Stripper Tip—*It's Not About the Bikini*—it would alter the way they approached business forever. This made me wonder what other advice I could share. What business lessons had I taken with me beyond the pole? And so began the makings of this book.

Honest hustling is imperative if you want to truly succeed in business, no matter what you're selling. It's about building long-term relationships and providing the absolute best products and services possible. It's about making a name for yourself.

And speaking of making a name, I've made a name for almost everybody in the book and disguised a few identifying details to protect the innocent—and the guilty. Although the essence of the stories is true, I've exercised a bit of creative license for your entertainment and to help make sense of it all.

This book is written from the perspective of the woman I've become. Not only do I have an additional decade of business experience, I've also helped hundreds of women entrepreneurs gain confidence, clout and cash in their own businesses. This book is titled *Think Like a Stripper*, but it could just as easily be called *Think Like Erika*. But what fun would that be?

This book has 68 Stripper Tips, each divided into two parts. Part I reveals the smart, productive and positive things I learned in the strip club. Part II, the Strip-Down, describes how each lesson can be applied to your own business.

Some of the Stripper Tips demonstrate how to do

business *your* way. Others offer suggestions to increase productivity and efficiency so you can gain measurable momentum in your business. And some of the tips will propel you to be a more creative and resourceful problem solver. If you apply and practice these tips in your business, you will up your confidence, attract more clients and rule your market.

So slip into your stilettos and step up to the stage. You're about to learn how to think like a stripper.

Erika Lyremark

STILETTO TRACKS

Each of my Stripper Tips is a story, but the stories aren't in chronological order. This will help you keep track of my travels and triumphs.

1971: Born in Minneapolis, Minnesota

1979: Began obsession with *Vogue* magazine

1990: Moved to Seattle, Washington

1991-2001: Danced in nine clubs throughout Seattle, Portland and Las Vegas

1995: Graduated with A.A.S. in Apparel Design from Seattle Central Community College

2001: Graduated with B.A. in Women Studies from the University of Washington

2002: Moved back to Minneapolis; became co-creator and managing partner of family-owned commercial real estate business

2005: Received Professional Coaching Certification from Adler Graduate School and became a business coach while still working in family-owned commercial real estate business

2009: Launched Daily Whip

2011: Left commercial real estate and went full-time at Daily Whip

1. Wake Up. Game On!

OWNING A BUSINESS REQUIRES OVARIES OF STEEL. GET USED TO IT.

Stripper Tip #1: *Always Have a Red Carpet Dream*
So how did a smart girl like me wind up flashing her boobs for crumpled dollar bills?

It all started with *Vogue*. Eight years old, sitting cross-legged on my bedroom floor, I would stare at page after glossy page of beautiful models hawking luxury products. I didn't know anything about what I would later deem "Red Carpet Dreams," but I knew I wanted to be a fashion designer.

I grew up in the suburbs of Minneapolis under the tough thumb of my conservative Christian family. (The chances that I'd grow up to be a stripper were either extremely slim or inevitable. Take your pick.) While still in high school, I moved out of the house and got my own apartment with a friend in the Uptown area of Minneapolis.

A few months after turning nineteen, I hightailed it out to Seattle with a group of friends.

My fashion-design dream stuck with me. After a few years of living there, I set my sights on an apparel design program at Seattle Central Community College.

Don't let the word *community* fool you; the apparel design program was notoriously tough. Word on the street was the program director was stricter than the Pope, ruled with an iron red pen and many of the students either quit or flunked out before graduation. For a Type A girl like me, it was perfect. With a Red Carpet Dream filled with runways, supermodels and full-color magazine spreads, I decided to enroll.

But there was a problem. In order to be successful in the apparel design program, I needed two things: tons of cash and tons of time. Working as a waitress would give me neither. My parents had already agreed to help by providing half of my tuition. (And I was well aware of how lucky this made me.) But because debt was a four-letter word I didn't want to use or abuse, getting a school loan was completely out of the question.

Call it coincidence, fate or something in between, but several of my friends at the time were working as strippers. They were not your stereotypical bimbo strippers with fake tans and faker ta-tas, but smart, savvy, studious girls like me. I'd meet them for drinks after work and they'd gloat about their exotic careers and the crisp hundred-dollar bills in their wallets.

Stripping is a job most people would never do, but the allure of fast cash funding my Red Carpet Dream—jet-setting across the international fashion world and having

Cindy Crawford and Linda Evangelista beg to model my latest designs—was too intoxicating to resist. I'd found my perfect school, and I had a Red Carpet Dream that left me shivering with ecstasy. All I needed was a new pair of stilettos, bulletproof confidence and an extra dose of courage.

The Strip-Down: Your Red Carpet Dream is the slightly terrifying vision that compels, excites and motivates you to take risks and step outside your comfort zone. It's your endpoint, your big finish, your Oprah moment. It's about waking up hot for your business every day, knowing that you have a mission. You have a purpose. You *can* impact the world and you *can* make money doing what you love.

If you don't have an I'd-do-anything-to-get-there end goal just yet, you need to take action fast. The world does not need another smart, motivated and magnificent woman living a prepackaged and predictable life. Stop wasting *you*. You are a precious resource. Somewhere inside your own gorgeous self, you have a lip-smacking good, glam-o-matic Red Carpet Dream. I promise!

Don't let your Red Carpet Dream live only in your mind. Get out a pen and paper and write it down. What turns you on? What have you always wanted, but never dared to dream about, until now? What seems impossible to achieve, yet you can't stop thinking about it? What gives you goose bumps and deep chills? Don't stop writing until you're feeling excited. That's when you know you've discovered your Red Carpet Dream.

Red Carpet Dreams can change, and they often do, not because the dream wasn't real and relevant, but because we all evolve and change. My Red Carpet Dream has transformed over the years from becoming a fashion designer to a women's rights lawyer to a real estate tycoon to empress at Daily Whip—and I'm sure it will shift again. Give yourself permission to revise and revamp it, but no matter what, *always have a Red Carpet Dream!*

Stripper Tip #2: *Count the Pros, Not the Cons*
My choice to become a stripper was not an immediate or simple decision. In fact, it was an entire year from the time I first thought about stripping until I actually did it. The thought of becoming a stripper was tempting on so many levels, but I needed to make sure my entrance into the underworld of exotic dancing was meticulously calculated. To help me make my choice, I decided to weigh my pros and cons. Here's what my list looked like:

Stripping: Pros

- Flexible hours
- Overcoming a basic fear (public nudity) would make me courageous
- Lots of cash
- Paid in cash immediately
- More CASH
- I am proud of who I am and judgment about my choice will only make me a stronger woman

Stripping: Cons

- Perverts
- Sleazeballs
- Potential family fallout
- Corny strip club DJs
- Long hours trudging around in six-inch platform shoes (permanent nerve damage?)
- Public nudity
- People will think I'm a whore and it will destroy any chance I have of legitimate, respectable business success later in life

On paper, the cash-heavy pros were pretty well matched with the public nudity-heavy cons. But, strange as it may sound, making that list showed me that I still wanted to be a stripper. Sure, I could have found another way to pay for college—millions of students manage to do it every year, while keeping their clothes on—but I knew that if I could get naked in front of strangers, I could achieve anything, like being the CEO of a Fortune 100 corporation, an elite fashion designer or even a benevolent dictator of a small country. I wanted to be an unstoppable force, and, at twenty years old, I knew that being chicken wouldn't help me achieve my Red Carpet Dream. Working in a strip club would do more than just get me cash. It would force me to be courageous and confident, and ultimately help me believe in my own capabilities.

My mission was clear. I was going to buck up and dress down. I would sacrifice my modesty to become the businesswoman I wanted to ultimately be: confident, bold and influential.

The Strip-Down: There will always be cons to your Red Carpet Dream: emotional risk, financial risk, the disapproval of your friends and colleagues, a significant other who feels threatened by your aspirations. Maybe you don't want to sabotage a great-paying gig. Maybe you're just scared of change.

The path to success isn't always sexy. So, why bother? Because you feel your Red Carpet Dream in your bones, and you've dreamt about it night after night, year after year. For a business bombshell, nothing is better than making loads of money doing what you love. When it comes to your Red Carpet Dream, cons aren't always bad—they are simply the individual challenges you defeat, one by one.

Have you sketched out your list of pros and cons? If not, take five minutes and do it now. Which cons on your list are secretly excuses for living small, or justifications to give in to your fears? Once you put your pencil to paper, you've taken a giant step forward in pursuing your Red Carpet Dream.

Go back through your list and brainstorm how you can bust through your cons. Are you excited? Are you inspired? Can you see your Red Carpet Dream unfolding right before your eyes? If so, you've discovered—and not a moment too soon—that you need to *count the pros, not the cons!*

Stripper Tip #3: *Create a Stage Name*

One unwritten rule among strippers is that you must adopt an alias. There are two reasons for this: 1) aliases protect the identities of the women whose offerings are on public display, and 2) aliases create a greater sense of theatrics that help put patrons in a wallet-friendly mood. I had a third reason: I was sure an alias would help me overcome my fear of public nudity. So when I knew I was going to be twirling around the pole, I stripped off my name, too.

But I didn't want to lose my unique identity in a sea of Savannas, a crowd of Madisons and a herd of Bambis. There was already plenty of Ginger and Cinnamon on the spice rack. I needed a stage name to represent my college-bound, goth-girl attitude; something equal parts fun and fearless.

On a piece of paper, I listed my essential qualities. More overt traits like *intelligent, funny* and *ambitious* hit the paper first. These were followed by *assertive, vocal* and *punchy*—an acknowledgment of my more masculine side. The image I wanted to project was that of a hot, sharp, edgy chick who wrote her own rules, was quick to crack a joke and was even quicker with the feisty backtalk.

Here are some of my initial name choices:

- Cool: Dorian or Dietrich
- Badass: Ursula or Natasha
- Sassy: Bianca or Paloma

I eliminated Dorian and Dietrich first. Even though I found the names incredibly sexy, I was concerned that the Average Joe would not. Ursula and Natasha were nixed for being too bold-sounding. I eventually landed on a sassy name inspired by Erica Kane's daughter on *All My Children* and my favorite character in the Disney movie *The Rescuers*: Bianca. These two antithetical associations were the perfect balance of sweet and evil.

Bianca represented the spontaneous, precarious personality that characterized my dancing career.

Occasionally, I'd change my stage name for an evening, or even for a few months. But I always returned to Bianca and her sexy, devious allure. She gave me confidence, superpowers and self-love. And when she went overboard on her sass? Not my fault. Blame it on Bianca.

The Strip-Down: Creating a stage name will help you break through obstacles. Even Beyoncé had a stage name to help her overcome stage fright! It's true; she created Sasha Fierce to differentiate her stage persona from her shy personality. And she's living her Red Carpet Dream!

Here's how you do it. First, identify where you are experiencing stage fright. Making sales calls? Asking for the money? Firing someone? Making a brave business move? Second, make a list of the qualities you want to evoke. Sassy, fearless, bold? Sexy and smokin' hot? Bitchin' and badass?

Third, pick a name that embodies these attributes. How about Princess of Power? Diva of Done? Mistress of Magnificence? Or choose a real name like Alexandra, Fiona, Daisy or Delilah. You can use the name of a movie star, or a revolutionary like Joan of Arc. Think of anybody—woman or man—who inspires you. Pick a name that makes you giddy, gives you courage and has you happy-dancing in your stilettos.

Create a stage name, and you can wear it whenever you need the extra skin and ditch it once your mission is accomplished. Or, you never know, you might love this new lady and want to be her all the time!

Stripper Tip #4: *Don't Work the Low End of the Stripper Pole*
Even though I was ready to buck up and dress down, I wasn't ready to quit my waitressing job and dive in to club life just yet. I needed a sneak preview of Stripperville. A friend suggested I be a peep-show dancer. A thick piece of glass would protect me from the customers, no one would be able to put their paws on me and I wouldn't have to work alongside fifty experienced dancers. It sounded like the perfect way to dip my toes into the shallow end of the stripper pool.

I lasted three weeks.

The eight-hour shifts left me drained and bored. Plus, the heavy stream of customers that I envisioned never materialized, and when the place did see a lot of customers, I was stuck inside a soundproof cage. The fact that I couldn't engage in any kind of conversation with customers until after they bought a show hurt my chances of cashing in. As a waitress, I knew that my humor and charm were substantial factors in the size of my tips. And the worst part of all? I had made more money waitressing!

Clearly, I was starting out too low on the stripper pole. In order to reach my Red Carpet Dream, I needed to become a *real* stripper, in a real strip club—not a half-naked mime behind a piece of solid glass. It was time to ditch the glass cube.

The Strip-Down: It's okay to start out at the bottom so you can gain experience and insight, but it's not okay to stay there.

If your current situation is starting to squash your potential—rather than propel it—stretch those creative limbs, change up your work schedule, revamp your business model or flip businesses altogether. As long as you're moving toward your Red Carpet Dream, taking the next step will not be a mistake but a necessary move forward.

You need to be excited about what you're doing, what you're selling, how you're selling it and to whom you're selling it. Eventually, if you're rolling out your Red Carpet Dream in the right direction, you'll need to upgrade your business. When that time comes, *don't work the low end of the stripper pole.*

Stripper Tip #5: *Big Girls Take Baby Steps*

I was finished with the low end of the stripper pole and nearly ready to quit my waitressing job and work in a big strip club. But I needed to give myself a few more baby steps to help me build my confidence before I decided to commit to the adult entertainment industry. So I entered an amateur stripping contest.

My first amateur contest was totally wild—Wild Turkey, that is. I was so nervous before the contest that I got hammered on Wild Turkey. Dancing to Alice in Chains' "Them Bones," I could barely stand upright onstage, and my stumbling, drunken performance didn't even place me in the contest.

After that experience, I vowed to always strip sober—a promise I kept for the first seven years of my new career. (As you recall from the introduction, the last two years were another story.) The following week, I trekked out to the edge of the city for another amateur contest. Even though I came close to flopping on my rear again—not from alcohol, but from my slick stiletto boots—I quickly regained my composure, made my way to the pole and incorporated the removal of my boots into the act. I twirled like a pro and felt in control. And I won first place! With two hundred dollars in my pocket and a blue ribbon to boost my confidence, I was finally ready to be a stripper.

The Strip-Down: Don't let your nerves run the show. If an impending business transition is overwhelming you, chill out and remember that *big girls take baby steps*. Nobody expects you to make a flawless leap. You don't have to perform like a pro your first day on the job. Whether you're changing businesses, lifestyles, Red Carpet Dreams or all of the above, relax!

You'll be more prepared for whatever happens next if you break down your goals into manageable baby steps. For instance:

Baby Step 1: The Stakeout: Keep your stilettos on the ground. No fast moves here. Invite some supportive and open-minded friends over for cocktails. Then take out your Red Carpet Dream and throw it out in the open. Prepare for questions and exclamations. But, most importantly, keep F-U-N a top priority.

Baby Step 2: Wiggle It (Just a Little Bit): Move a little faster. Maybe make a phone call. Maybe buy a domain name. Great work! Your stilettos have left the ground.

Baby Step 3: Stiletto Dancing: You've hired a business coach. You've been networking and asking questions. You even have a potential client. Now it's time to push yourself further and see how far you can go.

Baby Step 4: The Effin' Flying Leap: Eventually all big girls need to fly. So when you're done with Baby Steps #1-3, let the guardrails go and soar on your own.

Stripper Tip #6: *You're Already Naked, So Go for It*
Getting buck-naked at the peep show—usually for a crowd of one—was one thing; baring my birthday suit in front of hundreds of people made me feel like I'd swallowed a stiletto. I come from an extremely modest family. We never discussed our bare bodies, much less showed them off. By the time I turned twenty-one, the only people who had seen me naked—beyond the usual diaper changes and childhood streaking incidents—were my doctor, my one long-term boyfriend and a childhood friend. To say I was not a natural candidate for stripperdom would be the understatement of the millennium. I was completely out of my element. But there I was—center stage in the amateur contest—naked—in pursuit of my Red Carpet Dream.

Much to my surprise, no one booed, laughed, threw insults or tossed rotten tomatoes. Sure, no one got too excited, either. They didn't yell out, "Go, baby, go! Work it on out!" like in my favorite 1960s movie, *Faster, Pussycat! Kill! Kill!*

Holy cowbells, I thought afterwards, *being naked isn't that big a deal!* My thick layers of nudity-related fear disappeared. I knew at that instant that I had turned a

WAKE UP. GAME ON!

major corner and graduated to a higher cosmic level of understanding. Not because I had taken off my clothes, but because I had learned that fear is nothing more than a big plate of greasy lies we willingly feed ourselves. Instead of the awful, gut-wrenching scenario I had predicted, I felt no different onstage than when I was naked in front of my boyfriend. This was a truly awesome sense of freedom. And I was finally ready to commit to stripperdom.

The Strip-Down: The biggest obstacle standing between you and your Red Carpet Dream is fear. Fear tells you to play it safe. Fear broadcasts doubt and insecurity. But fear doesn't protect you or save you. Even legitimate fears are negative if they limit you from discovering your real strengths. We forget that since we *choose* to believe in our fears, we can *choose* to surpass them.

The best advice I ever received about getting over my fears actually came from my dad, a few years *after* I'd stopped stripping. Tenacious, smart and successful, my dad is an incredible entrepreneur. And so I asked him, "Dad, how are you so good at moving past fear?" He said, "Erika, I'm going to tell you my secret. I pretend that I'm on top of a tall building, and I'm naked. And everybody can see me. And I figure, I'm already naked, so I might as well go for it."

My dad's secret is absolutely perfect! *You're already naked, so go for it!*

Stripper Tip #7: *Put On Your Training Heels*

I was finally ready for the real deal. Over the previous months I had built up grit working the peep-show scene, found courage in my stage name and established a new level of comfort with public nudity. There was just one technicality in the way: I still didn't know how to give a lap dance. None of the strip clubs offered a stripper training program, so I needed to find a mentor to help me with my moves. Who better than my stripper friend Deanna, who had already been dancing for several years?

My first lesson with Deanna didn't begin with a lecture or a PowerPoint presentation. Instead, Deanna brought me into her living room, plopped me on her couch, got some tunes going and went to work explaining the intricacies of each technique. As she bumped and grinded on my lap, Deanna worked my body as if it were her own. When it was my turn to take the helm, all I could do was hope that some of Deanna's sensual skills had entered me through osmosis. After an hour of practice, she deemed me a good-enough lap dancer to not make a fool of myself. She also gave me advice on some of the finer points of the profession such as stage dancing, hustling the customers, working with the other dancers and dealing with club management.

Deanna's expert tutelage and unwavering support were priceless. Knowing I could rely on her for guidance gave me the confidence I needed to become a world-class lap dancer.

The Strip-Down: Starting a new chapter in your business life can leave you feeling awkward. No matter how unique your situation feels, there are people who have already been successful at what you want to do.

Once you have determined what skills, talents and knowledge you're lacking, seek out a mentor who can help fill in the gaps. If you can't find someone to help you for free, work out a trade or *invest your tips* (see Stripper Tip #31) to get the assistance you need. You can even look for mentors outside your industry. You might be operating different businesses, but many leadership techniques and business philosophies are universal. The more you *put on your training heels,* the more successful you'll be.

Stripper Tip #8: *Remove the Safety Net*
I'd taken baby steps, I'd danced in amateur contests, I'd moved beyond the low end of the stripper pole, I'd gotten naked in public and survived and Deanna had taught me how to lap dance. The only thing standing between my cash and me was my waitressing job. It was time to quit, but I was still scared. What if I couldn't make it as a dancer? What if I was the world's worst stripper? Even though I knew how to hustle as a waitress, I was terrified that those skills wouldn't transfer to my new naked gig. And, somewhere in the middle of all that fear, I knew that if I didn't remove the safety net, I would never find out what I could achieve. I needed some way to give myself the courage to finally take the effin' flying leap.

And then it came to me. Props! I went all out with my props so I could be physically and mentally ready to remove the safety net. Investing heavily in my gear, I ran to Nordstrom and bought myself some gorgeous lacy lingerie; a super-sized bottle of Fendi perfume; a pair of luscious, over-the-elbow black leather gloves—and I made an appointment to have five hundred dollars' worth of the finest hair extensions on the market put in, pronto.

I gave my two weeks' notice, left behind the certainty of a paycheck (not to mention free pizza and pasta) and took the effin' flying leap! I had no school loans, no credit cards and no backup plan. There was only plan A, and that was to be damn good at what I did and raise a ton of cash before school started.

The Strip-Down: If you want a successful business, if you want that Red Carpet Dream, then you need to be hungry. Hunger keeps you focused, helps you prioritize and makes you take chances you wouldn't otherwise take. When the rent's due and the wolf is at the door, you get extremely creative. For business bombshells, safety is a fairy tale. Money is made in the risks.

When it comes to your Red Carpet Dream, if you have nothing to lose, you have nothing to gain. If you don't work through the discomfort and the inconveniences and take massive risks, you'll never step out onto that red carpet you're dreaming of. And you know what that means? You'll be just another business wannabe. *Quelle horreur!* You need to *remove the safety net* if you want to make it.

Stripper Tip #9: *Serve. Don't Sell.*
Twenty-four hours after quitting my waitressing job, I walked into the club to work my first shift as a stripper. I put on my sexy, lacy lingerie, spritzed on some Fendi, strapped on my heels, brushed my hair extensions, double-checked my

makeup, checked in with the manager, gave my playlist to the DJ and then stood around wondering what the hell I should do next. I'd never known until that moment how quickly self-consciousness could turn into terror.

As the harsh reality of working the floor set in, I began to miss the security of serving pizza and pasta. I knew I couldn't sit around all night. Still, I was petrified! I needed to take action. What was I supposed to do? Then it hit me. I would just imagine I was back at my waitressing job, wearing my green polyester apron, khaki-pleated slacks and white buttoned-up oxford shirt, and ask the customers for their orders—except now the appetizer, the entrée and the dessert would be me!

"Hello," I said as I approached my first customer. "How are you doing? Are you ready for a dance?"

He gave me the once-over. "No, thanks."

"Okay, I'll come back later," I replied.

This isn't so bad, I thought. *He's still looking over the menu.* After asking my fifteenth customer for his order, I heard him say, "Yes! I would love a dance!" Wow! My attitude of service had worked.

After seven hours of being a "server," I made it through my first shift. Sure, some guys were rude, but so were hungry restaurant customers. I didn't hit the financial jackpot my first night, but I made more money than I would have made waitressing, and way more than I would have made at the peep show. More importantly, I had realized that a customer is a customer. Whether I was serving pizza or lap dances, a customer had needs that I could fulfill.

The Strip-Down: It's so easy to forget, when you're terrified of falling on your face, that the customer wants to be served. Period. In other words: It's not about you! It's about how you can be of service. Being of service takes the pressure off to say the right things or to reach perfection. Your customers just want to know that you're there for them and that you can help them. So *serve. Don't Sell.* And ask them what they need. Always make it about them. Your success, and theirs, will come easier, faster and be downright appetizing when you serve it up on a silver platter!

Stripper Tip #10: *Shake It 'Til You Make It*
One morning, six months after I'd quit my waitressing job, my lunch was packed, my outfit was pristine and every hair on my head was perfectly combed. It was my first day of apparel design school. As I walked the six blocks to school, swinging my toolbox of pattern-making supplies and extra-sharp scissors, I sang the *Mary Tyler Moore Show* theme song, like a true Minnesota girl. I was so proud of myself.

I had worked through my fears of public nudity. I'd taken a risk and had left my secure job for a totally unknown future. I had gotten comfortable with approaching customers, giving lap dances and performing onstage. And I had made enough money to cover a semester of my college tuition, plus expenses!

What I learned that summer was that getting onto my red carpet required lots of practice and persistence—and patience with my learning curve. I had to constantly *shake it 'til I made it.* So I took every advantage that I could to get the hang of basic strip club survival. Like working six days a week, working double shifts and performing in contests—including the wet t-shirt contest. The repetition really helped me to get the basics down, the way it had years earlier when I was practicing cursive, learning to ride a bike or memorizing flashcards. And once I had the basics down? I became a confident, courageous, money-making stripper.

The Strip-Down: Don't quit before you get there! Practice, persistence and patience aren't always sexy—and sometimes you might feel like you're going nowhere fast. Don't let your discouragement or slow growth deter you.

When we first learn to walk, we take one step and fall down. We get back up and do it again and again, and repeat it until we can walk. Well, growing a business is exactly the same. It's a lather-rinse-repeat process and you have to trust it. I've been following this formula for over twenty-five years now and it has yet to fail me. Just keep going. And *shake it 'til you make it!*

2. Sell It, Baby!

THE ABILITY TO SELL SEPARATES THE
WOMEN FROM THE GIRLS.

Stripper Tip #11: *Know Your Business Seductress Style*
The night I met Lauren, the new girl at the club, I learned a powerful lesson. Lauren looked more like a bank teller than a stripper, yet customers were practically lining up around the club to get a dance from her. She had the stage presence of a pet rock in high heels, and her costume resembled prison lingerie: white cotton panties and a white utility bra. I knew Lauren had a close relationship with one of the floor managers, so after a month of working with her, I begged him to tell me her secret. He laughed and said she was paying him to develop her hustling skills. He offered to coach me as well.

I had serious doubts about the manager's tactics, but figured what the hell. He told me I should tell the guys, "I may look like the girl next door, but watch out, hot fire burning inside!" I giggled. Not because it was sexy—far from it!—but because it was ridiculous. *Hey,* I thought, *What do I have to lose? This might actually work!*

Eager to bank like Lauren, I embraced my nonexistent inner girl next door, approached my "next-door neighbor" and whispered in my sweetest voice, "I may look like the girl next door, but watch out, hot fire burning inside!" He swung his head around and laughed. "'Girl next door,' are you kidding me?" Clearly this method of seduction was not the least bit believable coming out of my mouth. I gave myself kudos for doing something new and decided I was better off being myself.

Some dancers were naturals at playing the unassuming girl-next-door, whisper-in-the-ear types. Others posed as blonde, bubbly, good-for-a-ride types. Me, I was the no-nonsense, get-off-your-ass-and-let's-do-this-thing type, no matter what brand I was rocking. (See Stripper Tip #30: *Let Your Brand Hustle for You.*) My best hustling tactics were wit, charm and perseverance. I wasn't the girl next door, but I would be the girl in their face making money—without all the giggling.

The Strip-Down: Selling your products and services ought to feel fun and instinctual. If it feels unnatural, you're probably working someone else's seduction. If you catch yourself impersonating a colleague or a sales "expert"—*halt!* Their flair might close deals, but does their style align with your personality? Don't muffle your signature style. There is no other business seductress like you.

When you find your inner business seductress is making bank, look around and take note of what is working.

What did you say? What did you *not* say? What made it fun? What made it easy? Pay attention. When the universe gives you an answer, take the time to listen. Whether you consider yourself the Badass Babe of Business or the Business Girl Next Door, *know your business seductress style* and embrace it!

Stripper Tip #12: *Strap On Your Blinders*
Working in a strip club was like being inside an aquarium. There was no privacy or separation among the dancers. This fishbowl-style transparency had its advantages and it had its disadvantages. While it was great for monitoring which women were making money and which customers were ponying up the cash, the constant surveillance also led to massive amounts of self-doubt, insecurity and paranoia.

In my first few months, watching the veteran dancers constantly make bank made me want to crawl into the back corner of the club and die. The utter ineptitude I felt every time I looked at the bevy of tanned, big-boobed, highly trained pros ready to glide onto a lap at the wave of a twenty was paralyzing. I knew that if I didn't figure out how to compete with these women, my earnings would never match theirs.

And then one night, as I drew in a long puff from a cigarette, it occurred to me that my life's accomplishments had never been based on what everyone else was doing. (I quit smoking in 1999. Smart women don't smoke, and I encourage you not to do so.) When it was popular to dress preppy, I learned to sew so I could make my own alternative clothing. While my high school friends were spending their junior year picking out colleges, I selected chic dishware for my future apartment. Rather than staying home from prom because I didn't have a boyfriend, I went to the dance with my friend Katherine. (This was 1988, so—believe me—it was controversial to go to prom with another chick!) So why did I care now? It was time to stop paying attention to what everyone else was doing, strap on some imaginary blinders, give myself a crack of the whip and giddy up.

I accomplished this by focusing on my end goal: cash. I stopped asking other dancers how much money they were making. I stopped checking the dancer scorecard to see where I was placing in the race. When I kept my eye on my personal stash of cash, nothing else around me mattered. Self-doubt, paranoia and insecurity had no chance of getting into my head. From then on, I realized that the biggest competition I faced in that club was me.

The Strip-Down: Life is dangerously brief. There's no time to be voyeuristic when it comes to running your business, furthering your career or living your life. It's impossible to achieve your Red Carpet Dream when you're hung up on where you are in the race or how much money your competitors made last year.

If you've done your homework and created a Red Carpet Dream that has you feeling hot and sexy, relax and play your own game. Stop giving your power and your entrepreneurial future to someone else. Focus and take action on what you want today, tomorrow and next week, and you will succeed. Make it a habit to *strap on your blinders* daily.

Stripper Tip #13: *Put On Your Big-Girl Panties*

In the real world, if you walked up to a guy while wearing a bikini and five-inch stilettos and casually flashed him, he would either be shocked, deeply grateful or both. But things are different at a strip club, where the customers are like kids with the keys to the candy store. Rules don't apply, and roles are reversed. Suddenly, average guys (and especially less-than-average guys) are not only calling the shots, they're turning down dances from beautiful women who would never date them.

From the beginning, I understood rejection was part of the game, and most nights I weathered it well, hustling through the disappointment by keeping my eye on the cash. But, one evening, a customer shooed me away like a pesky fly. I'd been rejected all night, and his rude dismissal unexpectedly bulldozed my self-confidence. I started to cry and ran to the safety of the dressing room, where a group of supportive dancers embraced me like bikini-clad Mother Teresas. They'd all felt my pain before. One dancer, Jasmine, suggested I call it a night, go home, have a nice glass of wine and give myself some plus-size pampering. I took her advice, paid my house fee (the nightly rent each dancer pays the club) and left. That night, in the safety of a warm, candle-lit bath, as tears ran down my face, I had a moment of truth—the naked kind.

"Look, Bianca," I said aloud. "If you're going to be a stripper, you have to know that rejection is part of the equation. Every time you hear *No*, remember that *Yes* isn't too far behind. Buck up and put on your big-girl panties—even if they happen to be a lacy black thong."

Once I put on my big-girl panties, I was able to look

at the rejection objectively. Some guys would never like me and might not spend money on me even if I was the last stripper on earth. But, in the long run, I was stripping for my Red Carpet Dream. And that dream was worth the temporary pain of rejection.

The Strip-Down: Whether you're selling business insurance or Girl Scout cookies, rejection sucks. At the same time, rejection indicates effort. If you're not being rejected on a frequent basis, you're not taking enough risks. Many people don't take advantage of the opportunities that rejection provides. Here's a chance for you to improve your product, change your sales conversation or add in new tricks. It doesn't mean you need to dismiss your whole business. Every customer will have his or her own preferences, conclusions and criticisms. And each of those opinions holds the potential for you to earn or lose cash. If you don't learn from hearing *No!* over and over again, you'll continue to hear *No* more than *Yes!*

Where in your business are you letting the fear of rejection hold you back? *Put on your big-girl panties* and make the call. Send the e-mail. *Ask for the dance* (see Stripper Tip #15). When it comes to opinions, there is no right or wrong. And some people actually get off on telling you "No." The key to confidence is expecting rejection and forging ahead anyway. Focus on your Red Carpet Dream, and focus on "Yes!"

Stripper Tip #14: *Walk In As If You Have the Job*

After six years of being a stripper, I decided to up the ante for myself. I headed for Las Vegas. The employment requirements for most of the stripping jobs I had in Seattle consisted of having a heartbeat, limbs and a willingness to get naked. But the mega-clubs in Vegas were different. Many of them required dancers to audition. This threw me at first. I was slightly offended that, after all of my experience, I still had to prove my striptastic abilities like some wannabe showgirl. But I wanted to work at *the* premiere club in Vegas, so I had little choice but to audition. My ruffled ego needed some pampering, so I decided to treat the audition as a mere formality, a tiny crack in the road over which my five-inch stiletto would easily step.

At 11:00 a.m., all dolled up, I walked in as if I had the job and informed the manager matter-of-factly that I was there to audition. She gave me the once-over and told me to follow her. As we walked toward the dressing room, she gave me a quick tour of the club. Everything was more or less strip club standard—except the stage.

I was used to dancing on small stages with poles and brass ballet bars. This was a true catwalk with nothing but floor, and lots of it. My heart dropped. What would I do if I lost my footing and didn't have a ballet bar or pole to catch me? I'd never fallen, but I'd always enjoyed the security that the poles and ballet bars provided. I quickly put the thought of falling out of my head and rehearsed my mantra: *I already have the job.* I said it over and over again until the audition began.

Once I started my routine, I forgot about everything except the dance. I was moving and grooving down the plank, impressing hundreds of imaginary customers and bending my body just right, when I noticed my clammy, nervous feet were starting to slip out of my stilettos. Damn it!

Furious at myself for having worn shoes with no heel strap, all I could do was grip my toes as tightly as possible to buy myself a few extra seconds. No luck. I slid off my shoes and across the stage floor. Instead of buckling, though, I revisited my mantra: *I have the job! I have the job! I have the job!* I got my shoe back on and stayed on my feet to finish the dance.

Not only did the manager clap when I was done, she yelled out, "Hey, congratulations. Be here at 7:30 to fill out paperwork." I had known I had the job even before I auditioned, but it was nice to hear the confirmation. Fall and all!

The Strip-Down: If you don't believe you can get the job, make the sale or win the contract, no one else will, either. If you're confident before the sale, chances are you'll follow through with the same money-attracting charisma that will make people want to work with you. And the key to being confident is being cool and collected—not cocky and desperate—even if everything isn't perfect.

If you don't get the job or make the sale, find out why. If the objection is worth addressing, that *No* is an opportunity to help your client make the decision to do business with you. Sometimes they don't have all the information; sometimes they aren't clear on the benefits; sometimes they can't see how your product or service can help them. Tell them, so you can sell them! Simply *walk in as if you have the job*—and don't back down until your mission is complete.

Stripper Tip #15: *Ask for the Dance*

You might think that being a stripper is the easiest job in the world and that all I had to do was smile, look good—and show my ta-tas—and customers would throw their money down. And yeah, that did sometimes happen—but not often. Most nights, stripping was like any other unpredictable sales job. I might have been scantily clad, but I still had to *ask for the dance* and close the deal, over and over and over again.

I was prepared to go to *almost* any length to get paid. So with Gloria Gaynor in my head belting out "I Will Survive," I attacked the club floor like a starving fisherwoman. I carried a giant net, and every customer was a potential catch. No one was safe from my fishnets and hooks. As soon as a new customer came through the door, I was right there.

"Hey, you want a dance?" I would ask, politely but assertively. If he said no, I moved on, knowing full well I'd be asking him again later that night. I maintained complete confidence with every rejection, knowing that the more times "You want a dance?" came out of my mouth, the more chances I had to make bank.

I made it my business to *ask for the dance* and didn't take *No* personally. Once I removed the emotional element from my sales pitch, being persistent was no big deal. Sometimes, that belated *Yes* came because the customer appreciated my diligence and wanted to reward my enthusiasm, even though I wasn't his type. Sometimes they thought I was funny and unloaded their dough for more laughs. Other times men bought so I would shut up and stop bugging them—really!—a small price to pay for peace and quiet. And sometimes they approached *me* and asked for a dance. I was a dance machine and nothing could stop me from asking—except cash.

The Strip-Down: If you want to succeed, you can't hide behind your desk, your website or your Miu Miu platform pumps. You have to *ask for the dance* immediately and repeatedly. This doesn't mean you should sound like a broken record or craft some cheesy sales script. The high-pressure '90s are over, and your customers will see right through any pitch. So, how do you *ask for the dance*? Build relationships with your customers and offer products and services that rock the house. Go old school and pick up the phone. Create fun and impactful newsletters your clients won't want to delete the second they hit their inbox. Blog, tweet, make YouTube videos, amp up your PR campaign, speak at events, host a seminar or webinar, have an event with a guest speaker, create a digital product or even write a book—but your whole campaign needs to be centered on asking for the dance. Whether you're building your empire online, on the air or in person, you are going to have to *ask for the dance* again and again and again. So have fun. Be real. Be one hundred percent you.

Stripper Tip #16: *"Maybe Later" Means "No"*

Dancing is, first and foremost, a sales job. I heard a lot of "yeses." I heard a lot of "nos." But what I heard most of the time was "maybe later." I struggled mightily with this part of the job because I had a bad habit of taking the Maybe Later customers at their word. *Cool!* I'd think. *I'll just relax till it's time to dance.* That money, of course, didn't always materialize when those Maybe Laters turned out to be guys too wimpy to say no.

As someone who fancies herself a bright girl, it took me an inordinately long time to figure out that "maybe later"—even when delivered with an earnest smile—usually meant "No, I do not want a dance from you." When I caught on to this coded language, my immediate reaction was anger. How dare they screw with my livelihood? Didn't they realize that some people still took others at their word? In my vocabulary, "later" meant *later*, not *never*.

Behind my anger was a flood of insecurities. Was there something wrong with me? Was my body that hideous, or my personality that obnoxious? I mentally smeared my customers left and right for their thoughtless manners, and I wasted energy feeling sorry for myself.

It was precisely at that moment—when my self-confidence stood up and walked out the door—that I regained enough mental wherewithal to recognize that I wasn't, in fact, ugly or awful, and that every girl in the club was routinely getting the same Maybe Later song and dance from customers.

I promptly adopted a new ironclad sales policy. Anything other than a definitive "yes" was considered a "no," and heaven help the "no" people. (See Stripper Tip #15: *Ask for the Dance.*) Accepting that *"maybe later" means "no,"* I gave my full attention and energy to those who wanted a dance *now!*

The Strip-Down: Any sort of delayed response from a customer or prospect tells you that they're not interested, or you haven't sold them on your product or service. If they were sold, they would buy now. Putting stock in "maybe later" ain't gonna pay!

If your prospects are hemming and hawing, find out why. Help them work through their objections and concerns. Answer all their questions. If they still can't make up their minds, move on. Seriously. When it comes to making the sale, there's only one word I want you to hear: *Yes!* Consider everything else empty noise. Remind yourself that *"maybe later" means "no."* There are customers out there who need and want what you have, and they need it and want it right now. Your mission is to find them.

Stripper Tip #17: *It Takes Tricks to Turn "Tricks"*
One particularly slow evening, I decided to find myself a customer. I identified my target and plopped down on the chair next to him. I turned on the charm, trying to warm him up with the usual canned, small-talk questions. He was having none of it. He told me that while he appreciated my effort, he was only there to watch the dancers onstage. He would not be spending any money that day, and he asked me to leave the table.

Typically when there were so few customers in the club, I ignored such a request and kept chatting. Persistence, after all, was my most effective sales technique. This time I decided to change my approach. I would honor his request for me to leave, give him some space and return later in case his outlook had changed.

Two hours later I approached Mr. Friendly and *asked for the dance* (see Stripper Tip #15)—and he bought five! Shocked by his abrupt turnaround, I asked him what had changed his mind. He told me the dancers working that night were too desperate and he had become hungry for a dancer with a subtler, play-it-cool sexuality. You know, someone like me. Wow, did I have him fooled!

This unexpected development had me revisiting my mantra of persistence. I realized that I needed to read each customer individually and apply different tactics as necessary. If I had kept bugging that guy for a dance, I would have been perceived as anything but subtle. And, that night, subtlety paid the bills.

The Strip-Down: No matter how good your hustling tricks, there will be someone who just isn't biting. If you happen to know that a client is a great fit for your product or service, then it's *your* job to get creative in selling it to her. Hustling is not a one-size-fits-all proposition.

There is an art to the follow-up. Sometimes it's giving your *Maybe Later* and flat-out *No* clients some space to see what else is out there. Sometimes persistence works. Sometimes, "Hey, just checking in" works. And sometimes an "OMG, I know you said no, but you have just *got* to hear about the results my clients are getting!" is what does the trick.

Whatever technique you use, remember that when you offer an awesome product or service and are having fun, you get your clients in the mood to buy. And clients in the mood to buy are more precious than a room full of Christian Louboutins!

Stripper Tip #18: ***Pump Yourself Up to Pimp Yourself Out***
Working toward my Women Studies degree, all I wanted to do was learn, think and continue to build my vocabulary. (I learned eight hundred new words in two years. I carried flashcards with me everywhere I went! I even studied them at stoplights.) I loved being a student! And so, as you might imagine, I found it hard to get excited about lesser intellectual pursuits, like bikinis, platform shoes and typical strip club dudes. I had to pump myself up so I could get that stripper momentum going. Soon, I had developed a trick to jump-start my attitude before work each day.

Driving to the club in my '86 Volvo, I would sing aloud—really loud—whatever song came into my head, from Duran Duran's "The Reflex," to Sesame Street's "People in Your Neighborhood," to Metallica's "For Whom the Bell Tolls." Using my vocal chords to belt out bubblegum songs, silly songs and swaggery, tough-girl songs helped me loosen up and prepare for action. Once I grew bored with singing, I would have a conversation with myself about how filthy rich I was going to be by the end of the night. Before I knew it, I would be back home in my comfy pajamas eating popcorn and watching reruns of *The Mary Tyler Moore Show*.

Loosening up my tightly-wound self significantly increased my chances of a successful night. While the other dancers started each shift moaning and groaning about how much they didn't want to be at work, I was embracing my inner Zig Ziglar. I would even pump myself up in the privacy of the bathroom stall. I recall one chick calling out from the next stall over, "What are you doing? Are you smoking crack? Girl, give me some!" Alas, my personal brand of crack wasn't for sale—then.

The Strip-Down: Make it a habit to get physically excited about your workday. Create a playlist of your favorite "pump yourself up" songs. Sing and dance along before you start your day. You might feel ridiculous, but you might also have a breakthrough.

Never underestimate your power to *pump yourself up so you can pimp yourself out.* Rally the forces of the universe to scream your praises. Remind yourself that you're wildly powerful, super strong and utterly unstoppable! Dance in the buff, tell yourself you *own* it and collect coin like no other. Go ahead, look in the mirror and tell yourself how it's gonna be. Pump! Pump! Pump!

Stripper Tip #19: *Be Your Own Best Playmate*

My least favorite part of being a stripper was having the same boring conversation with different customers, night after night. When you're constantly meeting people for the first time, life can feel like a never-ending parade of small talk. Everyone wanted to know how long I'd been working at the club, how much money I made, did I like my job, would I ever date a customer, blah, blah, blah. OMG, it was so boring.

One especially slow evening, I pretended to be from the South just to entertain myself. Working a Southern drawl like I'd had it my whole life, I approached a fine-lookin' gentleman to inquire whether he'd fancy a good ol' fashioned, down-home lap dance. He looked at me and said, "My goodness, where have you been all my life?"

I said, "Sir, I've been in a tower waitin' for you to yell

up and say, 'Rapunzel, Rapunzel, let down your hair.'"

Impressed with my quick wit and Southern belle charm, he looked at me and said, "Wow! You're educated." (Hard to believe, but that's really what he said!)

I replied, "That's correct, sir. Now would you or would you not care for that dance?" Turns out he did—several times over. Whether or not he knew I was faking, this guy had lost himself in the character.

Obviously, I was on to something. I began exploring other characters I thought would appeal to my customers (and to me). From a financial and entertainment standpoint, it was a win-win situation and a new hustling trick. On any given night, an unsuspecting customer was just as likely to be approached by a British tart, a saucy Aussie, a randy Irish lass or a hot Eastern European exchange student as he was by the girl from the Midwest who'd just come from a potluck.

The Strip-Down: Okay, I realize that most of you reading this book are involved with businesses in which adopting a fake accent would not work for you (unless you're Madonna or Meryl). So don't take this tip literally—after all, this book is called *Think Like a Stripper*, not *Act Like a Stripper*. But here's the deal: we're all playing one sort of a game or another, so why not have fun? Remember *it's not about the bikini*: If you are having fun, you will make money. So why not have a little fun and *be your own best playmate* when no one is looking? Practice your fake Swedish in the car on the way to your sales meeting. Break out those Irish tunes every time you hit a stoplight. Add some spice and humor to your commute. Go ahead, do it! After spending your morning belting out foreign babble, you'll show up to your meeting ready for fun and ready to close deals.

Or, if giving yourself an accent isn't your thing, then find your own way to *be your own best playmate*. We can all find buttoned-up suits and excessive professionalism anywhere these days, but it's not often we see an Entrepreneurial Empress making coin on her own terms.

Stripper Tip #20: *Get a Comrade of Kick-Ass*

Mine was Peggy, one of the club's top earners. She had gorgeous blonde locks and a killer body. She was pretty quiet in the dressing room, so I had always assumed she was a snob. In fact, I had gone out of my way to avoid her, until one night when she offered me some tequila. How could I refuse tequila? (Despite the promise I'd made to myself to always dance sober, by year seven, drinking on the job was becoming a regular occurrence.) After a few shots, my disdain for Peggy grew wobbly, and before I could talk myself out of it, we bonded. You see, dancers are fiercely competitive, and most of the time it is smarter to work alone, but I knew Peggy and I were going to be *comrades of kick-ass*. We both loved to hustle, and our relationship was based on inspiring each other to work harder and earn more money—in all sorts of sassy and savvy ways!

Thanks to a secret stripper sign language that we had invented, Peggy and I could indicate to each other which customers had deep pockets and which we should avoid. Wiping the brow meant "Phew! Glad that one's over." Patting the right hip meant "Hurry up, this one's running out of cash!" Thumbs through the bikini strap meant "Seriously, stay away from this one!" Playing the game kept us focused and on the move.

Peggy and I also devised outlandish stories about each other to see if we could get customers to believe them. One time, while Peggy was showcasing her smooth, muscular legs, I whispered in her customer's ear, "You know why they call her Peggy, don't you? She's got a fake one. Can you tell which leg it is?" Peggy paid me back later that night by whispering in my customer's ear, "Best sex change operation I've ever seen!" Most customers laughed along with our banter, but some clearly did double takes.

When I started hanging with Peggy, it was the first time in all my dancing years that I could have just as much fun in the club as I did outside of work. (And you recall what happened when I was having fun, don't you? *Ka-ching!*)

The Strip-Down: Partnering with a comrade of kick-ass is a strategic tour de force for your business, especially if you are a solopreneur. *Get a comrade of kick-ass* you can rely on for ideas, support, brainstorming and feedback when you need help gaining clients, keeping them and making cash. Make sure that you align with a partner whose style and humor keeps you buzzing, strengthens your business and motivates your hustle. Even if you orbit different industries, compare notes regularly on what's working and what's not.

Today my comrades of kick-ass are smart entrepreneurs who keep me on my stilettos. Not only do they challenge me to outdo myself, they're on my speed dial, too. I'm never too old for a secret sign language or inside joke. Are you?

Stripper Tip #21: *Catch More Business with Honey*

When I was on the pole, it was well understood that the more closely you resembled Pamela Anderson, the more money you made. That was the rule—and Honey was the exception. Big-boobed, puffy-lipped *Baywatch* bimbo she was not, but somehow, athletic, small-chested Honey surfed out of the club every night on a giant green wave of cash. No matter how slow it was, that girl banked. When Honey walked through the dressing room door, you could hear the other dancers groan in the background. She didn't need to *strap on her blinders* (see Stripper Tip #12); Honey had no competition.

The other dancers and I were perplexed as to how Honey was able to beat the Pamela Anderson and Barbie wannabes at a game completely rigged in their favor. But, since I was also a 180-degree departure from Ms. Anderson's physical appeal, instead of watching Honey from afar (with an evil eye) like the others, I decided to befriend her.

The first thing I observed was that Honey was sweet. She was always complimenting the other dancers, and befriending—rather than belittling—the newbies. She never went ballistic on the DJs if they played the wrong songs. And with the customers, she was the ultimate girl next door. She was practically the June Cleaver of stripping! For the men at the club with cash in their pockets, Honey's demeanor was like a superpower. Show me the biggest egomaniac and the cheapest jerk in the club, and Honey could have both of them on the back couch begging her to take their money before the dance even started. Honey's sweetness influenced her customers, her coworkers and— undoubtedly—her bank account.

The Strip-Down: If you want to win more clients, you need to let go of your ego. You need to soften like a hot, buttery mall pretzel. People want to do business with nice people. Period.

So here's what you can do to lay the honey on thick so you can pull new clients toward you, rather than push them away. Think of something that melts your heart. How about a romping, roly-poly puppy? Now go beyond thinking about it and start to feel that puppy in your arms—lovely, soft, kissing you with precious puppy breath. When you start to feel that puppy is actually there with you, take it a step even further and imagine that you're getting paid large sums of cash to love that puppy. Now that you're feeling the love, it's time to *catch more business with honey*! You'll melt even the steeliest of hearts and turn your puppy love into dollars that taste oh, so sweet!

Stripper Tip #22: *Get Back On the Pole*

I never knew how much money I was going to make on any given night. Nothing could accurately predict the size of the crowd or their appetite for Bianca's legendary lap dances. Some nights would be a five-star, seven-course feast, while others more closely resembled a trip to Old Country Buffet. The money always evened out, but the short-term roller-coaster messed with my head. It took me awhile to stop getting thrown by the dips and turns and just put up with the ride.

This breakthrough crystallized one evening while driving to the club with my then-boyfriend, who remarked on my happy mood. I was in the midst of an especially dreadful series of low-cash nights, so we were both surprised that I was anything other than crabby and blue. I realized I was giddy because I was eager to get back in and fight. I had finally internalized the importance of treating each day as a new opportunity to make lots of money.

"Who knows?" I told him. "Tonight could be the night I dance for the richest man in the world. Probably not. But it feels a helluva lot better to think positively than to wallow in self-pity."

The Strip-Down: Being successful in sales includes the following: failures, flops, screw-ups, boo-boos and rejection. Setbacks are part of every success story. It's never a question of "Will there be hard times?" Rather, "How will I learn from them?" and "How fast can I get back on the pole?" Selling is one big trial and error. And it's guaranteed that you will fail at some point, but you'll also win at other points. Which is why you need to start fresh, every day, and *get back on the pole*—because if you're not selling, you're not in business.

3. Make Them Want You!

BEING YOURSELF GETS YOUR CUSTOMERS HOT AND BOTHERED.

Stripper Tip #23: *You Are the Muscle in Your Hustle*

One night, while I was straddling a young lad, the gentleman smiled, scanned me up and down and asked, "What do you think your best feature is?" Without a moment's hesitation, I replied, "My brain, of course!" I'm pretty sure that's not what he was expecting, but nonetheless, my response kicked his excitement up a few notches and my brain took his fantasy to regions he hadn't expected as he found out we had a lot in common.

For the next few hours, twenty-dollar bills flew out of his pocket and stuffed my garter belt. We spent the rest of the evening discussing politics, Western and Eastern philosophy and foreign films. We tested each other's ability to solve algebraic equations with no pen, paper or calculator, and practiced our French. (At the time, I was studying all these topics in college. Don't expect me to translate *Les Misérables* or tutor you in algebraic functions these days!) And when his cash was *fini*, I bid him *adieu*.

Because a stripper's basic tools are her derriere, her décolletage and her demoiselle parts, her mind is often overlooked. Outsmarting the customer takes bigger brains than boobs. Surprisingly, on many nights, the less attractive but smarter women were the ones who banked—because they had more muscle in their hustle than many of the bounciest blondes who were barely scraping by. Without a fully engaged brain, even the hottest, sexiest stripper could go straight out of business!

The Strip-Down: There are tons of businesses that do what you do. Tons. You're never going to be everyone's favorite flavor—no one is—but you can still have an intensely loyal group of clients who come back, time and time again, for *you*. I'm proof of that!

People will hire you if they like you and if *you're* willing to get creative in helping them solve their problems. In the club, I was creative with how I gave my customers a good time. And now I'm creative in helping my customers succeed in their businesses. But I don't let myself forget that there are thousands of business coaches out there. As the old song says, "It ain't what you do, it's the way that you do it." So don't hide your best assets: your brain and your ability to be creative.

You are the muscle in your hustle. Let your brain work for you!

Stripper Tip #24: *Free Samples Get 'Em in the Door*

Over the years I worked at more than a few clubs. One of them mandated the "Texas Tease"—a free, forty-five-second lap dance. Every hour on the hour, each dancer in the club grabbed a customer and gave him a sample of her wares. This freebie elevated the energy in the club, prompted customers to consider buying another dance and gave them a reason to hang around. It also pissed me off. I found it flat-out insulting to my stripperhood. I was there to make cash, not dance for free. Screw you, club!

I wasn't one of the cheeriest dancers on the floor at the top of the hour. In fact, I let these little Texas Teases sour my whole attitude. Then, one night, feeling exceptionally hungry for cash (and exceptionally annoyed over those wasted forty-five seconds), I had an idea. I knew that if I could create a new character—a rough-and-tumble ranch hand, perhaps?—I'd be more eager to saddle some cowboys. I asked our resident "cowgirl" Darla if I could borrow her cowboy hat for the Texas Tease, and my mood changed instantly. I let go of my whiny attitude and embraced the forty-five-second freebie for all it was worth.

Armed with Darla's hat, I approached each "cowboy" with the goal of blowing his mind to the point that he'd be fumbling for his wallet as soon as his seconds were up. Instead of resenting the dude who was getting my dance for free, I could now look deep into his eyes with the seductive passion of a woman who knows she's gonna get paid. This shift in my attitude marked a big boom in business. From then on, I used the Texas Tease not just as a marketing tool, but as a reminder to let loose of my mental strongholds and not take my job so seriously.

The Strip-Down: You can't assume someone is going to immediately fall in love with your business and whip out the cash. So make freebies a part of your business plan. There's no better way to entice your customers than by giving them a quick bite of your products or services. You're not giving handouts; you're tempting the masses with samples. Word-of-mouth is a powerful marketing tool, and if people love your freebies, they'll tell everyone they know. But you have to make sure your freebies are as good as your paid offerings, or people won't spread the gospel about you. Here are some ideas.

Service-Based Freebie Examples:

- A 15-minute coaching/consulting session that is super focused and based on specific problems you solve. I built my business dishing out free 15-minute business whippings. They were hugely popular and brought me a ton of business, because they allowed me to showcase my expertise, and they helped people see firsthand that I was the one who would solve their business woes.

- A 15-minute class in which you address specific problems. One of my clients had a website-review freebie in which she would make a screencast video about the potential customer's website and post it on her blog. This worked very well because she could have a one-to-one conversation with a potential client AND showcase her expertise on her own site.

Product-Based Freebie Examples:

- Mail out/drop off samples of your products. Then ask your potential client if you can have a follow-up conversation with them later, to ensure that your product is helping them solve their problem. You'll show that you are dedicated to helping them, versus someone who just wants to close a deal.

- Host an event. Give out samples of your products and offer a steep discount if they sign up with you that night. And, again, ask if you can follow up with them about your product to make sure it's working for them.

If you find yourself feeling stingy, take forty-five seconds and give *yourself* a Texas Tease to shift your energy and free your mind. Jump up and down, sway your hips, get your freak on, do the hustle. Let go of all the pressure and enjoy the feeling of working for free. The trick is to focus on what you *will* be earning, not on what you're giving away. So put a little fun in your tease because *free samples get 'em in the door.*

Stripper Tip #25: *You Only Need Two Bikinis*
For many years, I purchased my work uniforms of lingerie and costumes as though the department store were on fire. (In retrospect, I probably should have shopped with a bucket of water to douse my checkbook.) I had enough costumes to clothe the entire cast of Cher's Vegas Colosseum show.

Everyone envied my epic collection, but the truth was I had so much to choose from that I never knew what to wear. My wardrobe had turned into a time-sucking monster—which meant I was wasting time picking out what to wear when I could have been making money. And then, as you may recall, I discovered *it's not about the bikini*. Did I really need so much spandex, lace and leather in my life?

My wise stripper friend Carmella suggested I sell everything—costumes, accessories and shoes—except for my two favorite outfits. I was skeptical. I'd spent years accumulating the ultimate stripper-wear collection, and she now expected me to sell all of it? But Carmella knew I had a soft spot for making money. And she told me that when she scaled back her collection to only two bikinis, her customers didn't even notice that she wore the same outfits all the time. So really, why bother spending time, money and energy on something that wasn't making me money? It was time to let the purging begin!

The following day, I identified my two favorite moneymakers and brought everything else to work for the vultures to purchase. In just a few hours, the other dancers had devoured my personal inventory, leaving me with extra cash and a slimmed-down closet.

From that day forward, I no longer agonized over what to wear, and I never had more than two bikinis. My laundry chores were cut by ninety-eight percent, and I had more money, time and energy to spend on my Red Carpet Dream.

The Strip-Down: Take a look at your marketing materials. Have you spent thousands of dollars on brochures, postcards or notepads, only to see them wind up in someone's trash (or in your own, because they're outdated so quickly)? And don't even get me ranting about cheap promotional pens, ugly mugs, ill-fitting t-shirts and polyester baseball hats that usually end up in landfills.

Are you excited and energized about writing blog posts, updating your Facebook page or hosting webinars? Are the people on your e-mail list turning into clients? How much ROI are you actually receiving on your marketing efforts? What's working well, and what's not working at all? Remember, *you only need two bikinis* as long as those two are actually making you money. Then, and only then, add more—if your company needs it.

Stripper Tip #26: *Always Be Seducing*

Go ahead and laugh, but do you know what I love? I *love* a good infomercial. Especially the ones from the early 1990s. Tony Robbins? Yes, please! The Snackmaster? Who could possibly say no to making a pie from canned cherries and white bread when it's presented with so much razzamatazz? You'd have to be dead inside! So imagine my mind being totally blown when I looked around the club one night and realized that I was working in a real-time infomercial in front of a live studio audience. I practically got weak in the knees. But, more importantly, I played the infomercial angle to the hilt, and it helped me rake in the dough. (And I do not mean the white-bread variety.)

In the club, everything was programmed to seduce. Yes, there were beautiful, scantily-clad women everywhere you looked, but it was a lot more than that. The lights were low. The candles were lit. The music was pumping. The DJs told the audience who was onstage now, who was onstage next, which featured dancers would be coming to town and what time the Texas Tease would be happening. The managers and bouncers gave customers discount tickets to use on their next visits. It was a massive wall of seduction, perfectly priming our customers to buy. And it worked!

The Strip-Down: Think of a movie release. Before the film is even complete, you're seeing teasers everywhere. You see ads with "COMING SOON" across the top. Then you see the full movie trailers at the theater. The actors are on Leno talking about it, tempting you with movie clips, and every magazine is reviewing the movie. Of course you're going to see it. It seems like a natural, reasonable thing to do. This movie has become a part of your environment, and that makes it easy to be seduced.

Let your customers know what you're up to. Tell them what's coming up next. Give them a sneak preview. Be excited about the next product, the next add-on, and they'll be excited, too. To *always be seducing* means to make buying easy for your customers. Even if they weren't planning on buying, they do, because you've created a very natural and easy transition for them. The close is easy when your customers have already been seduced.

Stripper Tip #27: *Be Queen of Your Domain*
During winters in Minnesota, every boy and girl knows what to do when they see a massive pile of snow: scramble

to the top, push down any kids who have already claimed the peak and announce, "I'm king of the mountain!" It never lasts long; soon, another revolution occurs and a new kid stakes his or her claim on the snowdrift.

At the club, things weren't so different. Every shift I *worked like the rent was due* (see Stripper Tip #43). I made multiple rounds every hour, sitting down with customers and asking them to buy me a drink. (The club gave the dancers a cut of the money made from the drinks they bought.) When I wasn't making my rounds, I was greeting people at the door, chatting with the bartender or standing with my friends, because I wanted to be visible to my potential customers at all times. If they forgot who I was, I knew the other dancers would be on my money, an unacceptable defeat for this queen bee.

I did whatever I could to keep "on top" of my customers, going so far as paying my most trusted coworkers— whenever they weren't busy—twenty dollars to sit with my customers while I danced onstage, with the promise that they'd return the guys to me once I was finished. Even while I was dancing for a customer, I was keeping track of every single movement in the club and making saucy eye contact with other customers, letting them know they could be my next lucky guys. When I ran out of ways to verbally *ask for the dance* (see Stripper Tip #15), I would lightly brush a patron's shoulder as I walked by, then smile and giggle like I was thinking of him.

Maybe things are different today. With social media, blogs and newsletters, savvy strippers have all sorts of ways to snag customers, inside the club and out. Unfortunately, I didn't have that kind of technology in the '90s. All I could do was promote myself the old-fashioned way: face-to-face. And night after night after night, I was *queen of my domain.*

The Strip-Down: Shiny ideas, objects and offerings are everywhere. If you don't want your customers to get distracted, you must be relentless and impossible to ignore. Remind them who you are, what you can do for them and why they need you. Even if you've had a great sales day, even if you've had a great sales month, even if you've had a great sales year, always strive to *be queen of your domain.* In addition to offering high-quality products and services, never let your customers forget how much you rock!

Yes, you need social media. But you also need other approaches. Take your clients to happy hour. Go shopping with them and talk about business while trying on shoes. Treat them to power pedicures. Send unexpected gifts and congratulatory cards in the mail. Connect your clients with the right people, even if you make nothing on the deal. Lavish them with love and service. This will guarantee that you will *be queen of your domain* forever!

Stripper Tip #28: *Turn Your Customers On*

The club was already set up with a mood-to-buy atmosphere. But I knew that there had to be more ways to *turn my customers on* so that *asking for the dance* would be easier. So, unrelentingly, I brainstormed until I realized that my customers were probably rigged the same way I was: crazy about their passions.

Ah ha! If given a soapbox, I'd climb up and talk about

my passions (at that time they were fashion, feminist theory and the Chinese Cultural Revolution) for as long as my audience would let me have the floor. I knew I'd discovered a goldmine. I would turn my customers on by tapping into their passions.

This epiphany had me feigning excitement over whatever interests my customers had. From muscle cars to the NFL to country music to investment banking to duck hunting—no matter what it was, I got into it! I had more plastic in my smile than most strippers had in their boobs. And my approach worked. I had one wealthy fly-fishing enthusiast who would come see me every time he was in town to talk with me about pike, panfish, loops, rods, hook ratios, line tests and currents while buying dance after dance—and all it cost me was $7.99 for a book on fly fishing and a little extra-curricular homework. It was a small investment that paid off big; something that didn't interest me at all had turned into cash in my pocket. (Well, I had no pockets, but you know what I mean.)

The Strip-Down: Wanna strike gold? Then figure out what motivates and drives your customers. What are they passionate about? What do they dream about? What has them happy-dancing in their stilettos?

Customers are buying you just as much as they are your products and services, and they tend to do business with people who "get" them. When you can make your clients feel like the center of the universe, and you can help them get what they really want, you'll be able to *turn your customers on* forever. Cash in on that!

Stripper Tip #29: *Define "Stupid"*

My first summer at the club, I had two customers in town from Japan. When they found out I was getting my apparel design degree and saving money for a Japanese sewing machine, they went bananas! They told me they would buy dances from me all summer so I could purchase one of their country's finest exports.

Sadly, on their last night in town, one of them couldn't make it. So the remaining businessman brought a teddy bear in place of his friend and insisted that I dance for the stuffed animal. This was a first. Regardless, I was down for doing something different and proceeded to rock the world of the furry surrogate. Sure, getting freaky with a stuffed animal looked odd, but the bear and I had a blast. (And no, the photos are *not* available on the Internet.)

As I was counting my cash at the end of the night, one of the other dancers told me how stupid I had looked dancing for a teddy bear. My response: "I made money, and it was fun, so maybe you should reconsider your definition of 'stupid.'" She gave me a vacant stare and rolled her eyes. But after a minute, she agreed with me. She even went so far as to ask when those guys were coming back. Suddenly, dancing with the bear didn't seem stupid at all. Saying yes to dancing with a teddy bear meant I was saying yes to cash—you know, the main reason that I became a stripper. That's smart!

The Strip-Down: Let's be clear about what is stupid. Stupid is giving rowdy teenage boys fireworks, fake IDs and a fistful of cash. Stupid is continuing to spend time and energy on the parts of your business that don't directly impact your cash flow. Stupid is something dangerous, something hurtful.

And, bottom line, "stupid" is what people say when they don't want to admit, "I'm too scared or embarrassed to try it myself."

What business opportunities have you passed up because you didn't want to look foolish? Speaking at an event? Promoting your latest product on local TV? Blogging for your business? Asking your friends, family or colleagues for referrals or connections? *Asking for the dance?* Sure, going out of your comfort zone can make you feel a little silly at first, but think of it as the perfect way to gain experience and build your confidence. So, *define "stupid"* on your own terms, and you might just decide to make "stupid" part of your business plan.

Stripper Tip #30: *Let Your Brand Hustle for You*
As a flat-chested, fair-skinned brunette with college credentials, I didn't fit the stereotypical stripper mold. (I got big boobs *after* I quit dancing—more on that later.) For the first few years at the club, I embraced my distinction as the edgy misfit. My eclectic arsenal of stockings, garters, lace and leather made me feel like a superhero, and that helped me compete with the best of the Barbie types. During that time, I was reading *Siddhartha*, *Frankenstein* and *The Awakening*; watching and re-watching films like *The Cook, the Thief, His Wife and Her Lover* and *La Dolce Vita*; designing evening gowns and corsets, tailoring suits and hanging out in goth clubs. Most men went gaga for my alternative beauty-and-brains combo. I had many repeat customers, and I was happy with my bankroll.

Then, around year five, I started to burn out. To amuse myself at work, I started quizzing my customers . . . on their vocabularies. Seriously! I was that bored. All day at school I was using my brain and getting really pumped about the world-shaking things I was going to do after graduation—and dancing really paled by comparison. But the money was great, and I didn't want to give that up. I wanted making money to be easier and faster. I needed a gimmick, dammit. What to do?

One Friday night, watching Barbie doll after Barbie doll rake in the cash, I started to think that perhaps my brand had limitations. Maybe it *was* greener on the other side. Maybe my goth-inspired, smarty-pants hallmark was costing me money. I was hungry to become a standard-issue platinum bimbo who could make a quick sale. But the mere thought of it made me nervous at first. Was I crazy to ditch a persona that came naturally in favor of something that felt so out of character? Or did I just need to *define "stupid"* (see Stripper Tip #29) and see if it would make me feel ridiculous . . . all the way to the bank? What would my goth girls say about my switch to the other side? I mentioned my concerns to a trusted coworker, who said, "Oh, man. I'd wear a green wig with boogers in it if I thought it would make me more money." Sold!

I traded in my beloved black garments and leather accessories for blonde wigs, two neon bikinis, a bottle of tanner and a jar of glitter. Yes, I felt ridiculous. Yes, I felt out of my skin. Yes, I looked like a bimbo.

Yes, I soon found myself making a lot more money.

Thanks to my new bimbo brand, I felt rejuvenated. I no longer needed to have lengthy conversations to increase my income, and I was dedicated to my job all over again. I came to love my new cheesy look, and the neon bikinis became my standard work uniform, no different than the white oxford shirt, khaki pleated slacks and green polyester apron I had to wear as a waitress. Was I there to look like the real me, or was I there to make cash? I think you can guess my answer.

The Strip-Down: If you love your brand, if it amps your energy, gives you momentum and does your hustling for you, break out the Champagne! You've found the soul mate we're all looking for. However, if your brand limits your ability to make money, don't let clichés hold you back. The grass *is* greener on the other side, and you too can create a brand that will make the sale easier and faster—if you *let your brand hustle for you.*

Even if—and *especially* if—your brand worked well in the past, don't cling to what was. (Evolve or die, baby; which is the sexier choice?) Your brand shouldn't be exactly the same now as it was when you started, and if it is, it's time to worry. Your insights about your customer and your market should be constantly causing you to tweak what you do and how you do it. Now, I don't mean you should get a full makeover every three months, but let's put it this way: You're not still rocking the same belly-baring t-shirts you wore in the '90s, are you?

Start noticing brands that turn you on—even if they aren't related to your industry. What makes those brands so attractive? What elements are they using that could transfer to your own company?

If you're not sure where to start the rebranding process, get professional help from a branding expert. Your brand is the face of your company, and you don't want just any surgeon giving it a lift.

4. Strip Smart!

SOLID STRATEGIES ARE SEXY.

Stripper Tip #31: *Invest Your Tips*

Strippers can accumulate a lot of money. Like any naïve kid with cash to burn, many of them go out and spend every dime they have (and also every cent of available credit) on trendy clothes, epicurean delights, weekend getaways and a shiny new set of wheels. Maintaining this kind of lifestyle, a dancer can lose her money even faster than she earned it. But not me.

I was frugal, and as you may recall, debt was the four-letter word that offended me most. It wasn't until my fifth year of dancing that I finally broke down and bought a car. I treated myself to the tank-like European stylings of a used white '86 Volvo. Could I have found my way into a flashy new BMW? Of course. But I had a pragmatic financial plan.

Each week, I would add up the money I made and distribute it according to my very precise budget, which allocated funds for food, housing, tuition and precious little else. It was a constant reminder that I was dancing in pursuit of my Red Carpet Dream, not so that I could finance a lush life-style. I kept my eye on my Red Carpet Dream and invested the majority of my money in college tuition instead.

The Strip-Down: How much money do you need to invest to make your Red Carpet Dream a reality? $10,000? $100,000? $1,000,000? If you value your Red Carpet Dream and are committed to making it happen, you must invest money. Period. We're not talking Astroturf dreams here, we're talking Red Carpet Dreams. Ladies, believe me when I say that I understand the necessity of Louis Vuitton bags and Jimmy Choo heels. But if your budget requires you to make a choice between the two, go for the Red Carpet Dream, not the shopping spree! I know it's a painful decision to make, but you'll have oodles of money for those indulgences later.

The intrinsic value of loving your business, believing in its potential and doing it your own way is utterly immeasurable. But you can't make your mark if you don't invest cash. So what do you need most? A business coach? An entrepreneurial strategist? A gorgeous website? A virtual assistant? A marketing makeover? A housekeeper, so you can focus on your business chores? What's it going to take for you to reach your Red Carpet Dream? The right services, products and people are out there, waiting for you to *invest your tips*. Do it!

Stripper Tip #32: *Adopt a Stripper's Business Plan*

On Sandra's six-month anniversary of working at the club, she asked me if I could answer a few questions she had about the business of stripping.

"Sure, babe," I said. "What do you want to know?"

"Well, I'm a business major, and we're learning how to make business plans at school. I heard that you've been dancing for seven years and I was wondering if you ever mapped your business plan."

"Yes, I did!" After my original excitement, I sighed. "But nothing ever turns out the way you think it will—especially not in a strip club!"

My original business plan was to:

- Make enough money to pay my college tuition.
- Dance for two years.
- Get my apparel design degree.
- Quit the stripping business.
- Become a world-famous fashion designer.

On paper, it looked so simple. Here is what actually happened:

- I made enough money to pay my college tuition.
- I got my apparel design degree.
- I did not quit the stripping business (or become a world-famous fashion designer) and instead began working on a Women Studies degree so I could become a women's rights attorney.
- Seven years later, I was still stripping.

"Here's all you can count on," I said to Sandra. "Some nights you'll make gobs of money and other nights you'll make jack. Other than that, it's all a mixed and unpredictable bag of fun, cash and creeps. Nothing has turned out exactly the way I had planned."

"So, in other words," Sandra said, "put on your push-up bra, slather on some tanner, whiten your teeth, have fun and make plenty of cash?"

"Yes! Now *that's* a business plan!"

The Strip-Down: Creating a hardcore, in-depth business plan is a superb idea. It will force you to identify what you want in your business, what you don't want in your business and any loopholes in your plan. It will also help you develop your revenue models.

Once you have your business plan, shrink it down to a loose one- or two-page outline that you can easily update every thirty to sixty days. Creating short-term business plans—as opposed to locking yourself into a narrow, long-term plan—offers you the flexibility you need for growth. In most situations, planning beyond three months is challenging, because too many aspects are unpredictable. Instead of "What if?" you'll hear yourself saying, "I will," and you'll follow through with greater frequency.

Along with this flexible approach toward the future, your business plan needs to be based upon a firm understanding of your values, idiosyncrasies, passions and strengths. When you *adopt a stripper's business plan,* your identity and your sanity remain intact. Remember that documents, agendas and lists are not meant to limit or strangle your ambitions; they're there to create structure and a support system for you so that you can live out your Red Carpet Dream! And, most important, remember that it's a business plan—not a life preserver.

Stripper Tip #33: *Resist the Sweetness of a Sugar Daddy*
In all my years of dancing, I never had the kind of customer who would lavish me with diamond earrings, French perfume, designer handbags or cute new outfits. That was fine. Having a sugar daddy would have meant having to spend time with him inside the club and out in the real world, too. Nothing is free, and even gifts have their price.

I never let my customers think that, by giving me large amounts of cash or luxury items, they would have a chance to date me or sleep with me. My life outside the club was my own. I kept even my best customers at a distance, and although I missed out on making guaranteed money, I was able to wake up every day knowing my life belonged to me.

When the topic of sugar daddies comes up, I always think back to a dancer named Tabitha, who rotated between three paying papas. They filled her purse with goodies, but she paid a hefty price for their attention. Regardless of whose night it was, Tabitha would spend hours lap dancing and talking with them on the couch, arms looped, like they'd been in love forever. She told me that she hated it and was dying from the soul-crushing boredom of sitting hour after hour, year after year with the same three dudes.

Me, on the other hand? I was out to hustle money from dudes, too, but I enjoyed myself most of the time. I could move around the club as I pleased, lavish attention on whomever I wanted and be the girl I wanted to be. The lesson here? You can't put a price on entrepreneurial freedom.

The Strip-Down: The power needs to be in your court. And whether you have outsiders wanting a final say in your business affairs or someone's got the expectation that you will abide by their ideals and standards, your Red Carpet Dream can quickly turn into a black shag nightmare.

Unless you are masterminding a multimillion-dollar business and you plan on taking your company public, finance it yourself. By financing it yourself, you'll be forced to think more creatively and resourcefully. The best ideas and businesses are born from necessity, determination and creativity. You'll lose money on some ideas and make bank on others, but nobody else will be responsible for your business except you. The best part of financial independence is that you don't need someone else's permission to shift your business plan. So if you want to do things your way and have full control of your Red Carpet Dream, *resist the sweetness of a sugar daddy*.

Stripper Tip #34: *Business Before Pleasure*

Each club where I worked had its standard dance fees, and that's what I charged most customers. But sometimes a longtime customer would want me to cut him a deal on a series of lap dances. Sometimes friends would stop by the club and want dances, and I felt awkward charging them full price. Sometimes it was a slower-than-sloths night and I was in the mood to wheel and deal, but I just didn't know what that "deal" should be. Each time it happened, I wasted a lot of time and energy negotiating my transactions all over again.

Then one night, while watching the classic 1970s movie *The Happy Hooker*, the other stiletto dropped: I needed to draw from a "sister profession." (You know, the one that, unlike stripping, involves doing the Triple-X with customers.) Prostitutes always make their customer "pay before they play," and they always negotiate what the transaction will entail *before* the transaction takes place.

I knew that by committing to *business before pleasure* I could avoid those awkward negotiations. I needed a clear-cut policy for my prices and services, the kind all good ladies of the night used. I would name my price, and customers could take it or leave.

While the clubs wouldn't permit me to collect the money up front, I created my own happy hooker price and service menu in my head. I had one menu for longtime customers, one for friends and one for when I needed to advertise a blue-light special. I let all my customers know my prices from the get-go. Business before pleasure meant a win-win situation. My longtime customers got consistent deals, my friends could purchase dances without any awkwardness and I felt confident discounting my services on those nights when it was the only way to walk out with something in my pocket besides lint.

The Strip-Down: It's important to have a warm and friendly rapport with your clients, but the essence of your relationship is business. Business must come before pleasure—any other way and you'll devalue your worth.

The best way to guarantee you'll get paid what you deserve (and save time and energy) is to be upfront and firm about the terms of your contracts, timelines and payments. It's okay to give discounts or have a sale, but set those arrangements up in advance—not on the spot when your customers (or friends) are smiling ear to ear with that please-make-me-a-deal look. Most of your clients (and friends) are in the dark about how to strike a deal. Fortunately, a strict policy of *business before pleasure* will light the way!

Stripper Tip #35: *Bring Your B-Cup Game*

It seemed like every time a dancer got a new pair of store-bought boobs, she was jiggling into the club to show off her updated rack before the bandages came off. Like a proud mama showing off her twin tots, she'd whip the girls out for the requisite *ooh*ing and *ahh*ing. Those of us in the A- and B-Cup Club were left to wallow in self-pity.

Given this bevy of boobies, you might think my own super-sized ta-tas were augmented while I was dancing, but you'd be wrong. I had itty-bitties the entire nine years I danced. I wasn't interested in having fake boobs as a stripper. Sure, I was a hustler's hustler and certainly having double-Ds would have made me even more money. But I drew the line at fake boobs and tanning. If I was ever going to get breast implants (or tan) I wanted to do it for myself and not to make more money or get attention from my customers or boyfriends. I knew I could still be proud of my skin and feel strong and sexy without tremendous twin tots for support. Eventually, augment I did, but not until four years after leaving the industry. (And, just for the record? I love my new girls!)

I didn't just accept my smaller boobs; I built a business

around them. I learned to be creative and persistent—skills
that have taken me very far in my career, and skills I may
not have needed to develop otherwise, had I not *brought my
B-cup game.*

The Strip-Down: You may not fit the stereotypical image
for your industry. But that's no reason to get discouraged!
The name of the game is bootstrapping, being resourceful,
thinking on your feet and getting creative. It's about using
what you have and making epic stuff happen. Bootstrapping
will improve your business skills and it will also make you
better at . . . well, everything. Thanks to the bootstrapping
I've done, I make quicker, stronger decisions and am more
creative. I've learned a bit about everything it takes to run a
successful business. And, big picture, it's allowed me to be of
better service to my clients, since I can now help people who
struggle with the things I used to struggle with.

For more ideas on how to *bring your B-cup game,*
read *Shark Tales* by Barbara Corcoran, founder of Corcoran
Group—one of New York's premier real estate brokerages—
and star of ABC's hit show *Shark Tank.* In a brilliant move,
Ms. Corcoran used high fashion to help herself bootstrap.
She spent her very first commission check on an expensive
coat from Bergdorf Goodman, so that she could give the
impression that she was, in fact, already at the top of her game.

Stripper Tip #36: *Upgrade to Double-Ds*
On slow nights, a lot of the women in the club would set
aside their competitive natures to work in teams. They

would happily double-up on lap dances on those nights, but most of them approached it backwards. They would find an interested customer first, and then grab either a friend or the nearest dancer to perform with them. On the other hand, I was strategic about working the lucrative threesome dynamic and would only double-dance—aka "Double-D"—with women who were hustling pros, women who could help me make it look like we'd been a terrific tantric tandem our whole lives.

My first partner was Malibu. In many ways, she was the complete opposite of me. If she was Samantha from *Bewitched*, I was the evil cousin Serena. She was a petite, muscular blonde to my tall, slender brunette. She listened to classic '70s rock 'n' roll, and I listened to gothic and industrial music. She was the girl every boy's mother wanted him to bring home, and I was the girl your momma told you to avoid. Together, we were the garden of good and evil.

What we did have in common, though, was that we were both Grade A hustlers. Our powers doubled when we worked together. Did Malibu need me to make money? No. Did I need her? No. Did teaming up put a new spin on our hustle? Absolutely! I gathered numerous referrals from my new "business partners"—an uncommon practice in such a cutthroat environment—and I was making more money and having more fun. Profitable teamwork? Who knew?!

The Strip-Down: In the business world, Double-Ds are known as strategic partnerships or joint ventures. This means that the person/company you want to partner with has the same target market, and you will both benefit when you align forces.

Double-Ds give your business a whole new degree of creativity and momentum. But remember, every partnership is an energy exchange and an investment. If you aren't profiting from the team play, keep it a solo act. If you're thinking of getting into business with anyone, take your time and do it right. And please, please, seek professional advice from both a seasoned CPA and an experienced attorney, always have an exit plan and start your partnership with paperwork. And don't forget the tip from the movie *The Happy Hooker*—knowing the deal in advance makes for the smoothest transaction.

Red Carpet Dreams are major commitments. You need to be deliberate with your time and energy. This is easier when you're surrounded by people who are as smart, successful and driven as you. Don't waste time or energy on anyone who just wants to ride along on your Red Carpet Dream for free. Find someone whose ambition matches yours and *upgrade to Double-Ds.*

Stripper Tip #37: *Think Outside the Candy Box*
The Candy Man was a jolly customer who always brought us sweets. He never said anything mean about anyone and was more than willing to lend an ear to our problems while we stuffed our faces full of delicious sugar. The Candy Man knew how hard we worked and did everything (with the exception of buying dances) to help us get through the night in high spirits.

One slow evening, I got up to use the restroom and he shouted, "Hey, Bianca, you forgot something!" I looked down at where I'd been sitting and sure enough, I *had* forgotten something—a caramel flattened by my tush! I instantly saw a moneymaking opportunity. I made a bet with the Candy Man that I could sell caramels that had been personally squashed by the illustrious Bianca. Selling price? Five bucks! He laughed and said he would match whatever I earned selling my signature caramels that night, dollar for dollar. It was on!

I then proceeded to ask every customer in the club if they wanted to buy a caramel warmed by my sweet cheeks. Some of them were so amused that they upgraded from a caramel to a lap dance. Between the $100 I made selling caramels, the price match from the Candy Man and the extra money I made from my sugared-up customers, the night didn't turn out half bad.

Obviously selling squished caramels was not my standard *modus operandi*, but in a pinch, it served me well. It gave me a unique opportunity to connect with my customers, provided cashola on a night when my chances of banking appeared slim and it just might be the most overlooked (and, until now, under-publicized) marketing strategy in the history of caramels.

The Strip-Down: Don't keep yourself prepackaged, and don't limit your ability to make money to "business as usual." *Think outside the candy box!* Revamp your business model, even if everyone thinks you're crazy; raise your prices, even if the thought makes you feel like you are going to hurl your green smoothie; ditch unsuccessful products and services that have been staples in your business since day one.

If you're not excited about what you're doing or how

much cash you're rolling in, think bigger than candy canes and lemon drops and allow your cash potential to expand.

Stripper Tip #38: *Be Blonde for a Buck*

Sitting back with a customer after a series of lap dances one night, I watched the dancing on the main stage. My friend Claudia was performing, and I commented on what a remarkable dancer she was. My customer replied, "Oh, she's okay, but I prefer blondes like you. You're natural. I like you because you're real."

I shifted in my seat, adjusted my blonde wig and grinned. "Yep, I'm all real, that's for sure." How a cheap blonde wig could dupe so many guys was a mystery to me. It couldn't have been more fake, yet night after night men complimented my golden locks. This conversation triggered an experiment.

I found Claudia in the dressing room afterwards and told her about my customer's blonde fetish. "Put on my wig and see if he buys a dance from you," I told her.

Claudia snickered. "Hell, yeah! I asked that guy for a dance earlier and he turned me down. Said I wasn't his type." I put the blonde wig on Claudia's head. It looked even more unnatural on her, which made the experiment all the more enticing.

Claudia waltzed onto the floor. When she returned to the dressing room, it was with a big smile on her face. "That gentleman definitely prefers blondes. He just bought three dances." On hearing this, one of our comrades, Annie, yanked the wig off Claudia, made a quick adjustment and zipped out of the dressing room. Fifteen minutes later, she was back. Sure enough, our customer had bought dances from her, too. I declared my experiment a resounding success.

The Strip-Down: Give your customers what they want in a way that aligns with your business, whether that means iPhone apps, "Tweet This" buttons on your website, less packaging for products, packaging that's biodegradable or—if you run a hotel, for example—organic cotton sheets that are washed as needed. Your customers are fickle and can be easily seduced by any passing little offer. So you need to be willing to *be blonde for a buck.*

A perfect example of a company that is being blonde for a buck is Red Stamp. This greeting card company offers paper correspondence and techno-correspondence via a gorgeous iPhone app they created for elegant texting. With their service, you can text, e-mail, post to Facebook and Twitter or mail a postcard through the good old USPS. Brilliant!

If you want to succeed, you must be expansive and ready to change when the market requires it. Rollercoaster technologies, economies and politics all dictate that anticipating and maneuvering change is a necessity for business growth.

Stripper Tip #39: *Following the Rules Won't Make You Rich*
The first club where I worked required an employment contract. Upon reading it, I was tempted to hire a team of attorneys to help me decipher what it said. The contract was lengthy, complex and restrictive, but I was hell-bent on being

a dancer, so I signed it.

For the first year, I followed every rule in the contract, no matter how minuscule. But the more time I spent at the club and the more familiar I got with its underpinnings, the more I saw the game for what it was. I noticed that certain women consistently failed to pay their house fee, certain women worked less than the required number of shifts and certain women got away with all kinds of seedy—and prohibited—behavior. Yet none of these women could get fired with a torch. I decided to test the boundaries myself.

I stretched the first rule when dancing to Tina Turner's "Private Dancer." Even though club management hadn't outlawed it yet (like they had gangster rap, hardcore punk and speed metal) the general rule was to only pick songs that would put customers in the mood to spend money. This groove-worthy song—classic for its guilt-ridden lyrics— would make any man feel ashamed for spending his time in a strip club, and could send him looking for ways to do penance. Sure enough, the moment I approached the tip rail, gyrating to the guilt-ridden beats, customers whipped out one-dollar bills like I was offering way more access to Bianca for way less cash, if you know what I mean.

My "Private Dancer" routine worked for a good month until a regular customer finally complained that the song was not appropriate for a strip club, prompting my manager to pull me aside and tell me that the song was officially banned. I wasn't heartbroken; the club had thousands of songs to choose from. What mattered was that I had broken the rules to my benefit—without repercussions.

The Strip-Down: First of all, I'm not talking about breaking any laws: this is about not adhering blindly to industry protocols. Innovate! *Following the rules won't make you rich.* If it did, everyone would be swimming in pools made of greenbacks. Trust yourself. Do your own thing. Be your own guru! One great example? Look at Zappos and their innovative free-returns policy. At the time, that was a massive rule-breaker.

So here's a little exercise for you: I want you to make a list of ALL the business/industry rules you've run across that you think are stupid and make no sense, but that everyone tells you you should follow. Write them down. (I promise no one will swoop down, look over your shoulder and call you out for disagreeing! You can even tear the list up afterward if you want.) Look at each one of them, and decide that you're not going to worry about it anymore; you're going to dictate your own moves and be done with it. Don't agonize over what so-and-so says you MUST do if you want a successful business. Know what works for YOU, and do that. (And yes, if anything I say falls into that category, so be it!) You're the boss. Act like it!

Stripper Tip #40: *Communicate About the Cash*
Strip clubs are an alternate universe where the market doesn't matter as much as the moment. Customers are not thinking with their brains. Under these circumstances, I could get away with just about anything.

It was commonly accepted that when a song ended, you would simply say, "Do you want another dance?" We would *not* remind them that each dance cost money and, thus, the meter would continue to run. I didn't want to interrupt the mood, or my cash flow, by calling attention to a client's budget; instead, I wanted him to enjoy (and pay for) dance after dance. When presented with the tab, the customer either knew the score or was too afraid of the three-hundred-pound bouncer to argue.

Until the night this hustler got screwed. On that fateful evening, I happened upon a real live wire and danced ten straight songs for the guy. I finally stopped and informed him that he owed me $200, at which point he went into a state of advanced sticker shock.

"Two hundred dollars? I thought the dance was twenty!"

"It is," I said, "and you got ten. That's two hundred bucks."

"No way!" he argued. "You only did one dance for me. I assumed you would stop when it was over. You can't expect me to stop the ride. You're the operator. No way I'm paying two hundred dollars."

This guy knew ten songs had played from start to finish—he had sung along as though it were a karaoke contest! But he wouldn't pay up. My manager approached him, and after a few heated words, the man suddenly turned and made a beeline for the front door—without paying for my services. I was pissed about the lost money, but I realized that in the game of stripper roulette, there were going to be times when I was going to have my hand slapped hard if I wasn't willing to *communicate about the cash*.

The Strip-Down: Business is about money. So if you are not willing to *communicate about the cash*, don't be in business. I know it can be uncomfortable, but if you don't master cash communication, you will never reach your highest potential as a business bombshell. This doesn't mean you'll *always* get paid; this means you're able to have a conversation about the money as easily as you order a dirty martini at happy hour.

Quick tip. Remember your *stage name* (Stripper Tip #3)? Use one if you know you need to have that conversation and you're terrified. How about Chatty Cashy? She loves to talk about money more than anything else. She LIVES to talk about money; the stickier the issue the better. And remember, like all business hustling, the more you do it, the easier it gets.

Stripper Tip #41: *Know When to Leave Las Vegas*
In Stripper Tip #14, *Walk In As If You Have the Job*, I told you about the time I decided to head for Vegas to see how I would do on the biggest stage of all. Well, after I got the job, here's how it all went down.

For years, I'd heard stories from strippers who had traveled to Las Vegas to work. Their daring tales made me feel like I was missing out on fun and cashola. I wanted to go, but none of my stripper friends were Vegas types. However, about six years into my career, I finally met some traveling-to-Vegas veterans I knew I could tolerate. I asked them if I could come along on their next trip. And so, a few months later, I was in Vegas, baby!

Yet only two nights into my work-cation, I wanted to go home. I didn't like working with hundreds of other dancers; I felt like I was working in a stripper strip mall instead of a cozy boutique. The enormous club was overwhelming. And I made the same amount of money in Vegas as I had made in Seattle. I realized that I had liked working in my hometown, where I knew the management and the dancers. I had made enough money on a consistent basis to support my needs and pay for tuition, and I got to sleep in my own bed at night, leaving my stripper life behind at the club.

Going to Las Vegas was a smart—albeit expensive—move. I went on an adventure, gave it my best whirl and realized that being a stripper in Vegas wasn't my cup of cash. So on that second day, when my shift ended at 3:30 a.m., I picked up the payphone and booked a 6:00 a.m. flight back to Seattle.

The Strip-Down: What have you secretly been wishing you could give up, even though you've paid lots of money to make it happen? A new website? A new product or service? A new office space? It can be hard to let go and change lanes. But this is not about quitting on yourself. It's about redirecting your Red Carpet Dream.

Even if you've paid the money, signed on the dotted line, moved all of your belongings and changed your address, if what you're doing isn't in alignment with your Red Carpet Dream, redirect that carpet—and fast! It's good to *know when to leave Las Vegas*; that's what smart entrepreneurs do.

5. Keep It Simple, Sexy!

GOOD NEWS: WHEN YOU WORK FOR
YOURSELF, YOU'RE THE BOSS.
BAD NEWS: WHEN YOU WORK FOR
YOURSELF, YOU'RE THE BOSS.

Stripper Tip #42: *Crack Your Own Whip*

One of the strip clubs where I worked had no set schedule. You could come and go as you pleased. As long as you paid your house fee and there were enough women to entertain the customers, the club management didn't care when or how often you worked. The freedom was fantastic, but the loosey-goosey structure made it easy for certain women to lose their motivation and become less accountable.

My friend Penelope was one of those women. As much as I loved working with her, it rarely happened because she was a master at finding reasons not to show up. "Oh, it's too windy," "I might be getting my period," "I ate garlic last night and might have bad breath" and "There's a good movie on Lifetime that I want to see" were all fair-game excuses for

Penelope. With no boss forcing her to work, she was a slave to her own laziness. I, on the other hand, had a boss who went by the name of Red Carpet Dream, and she was a sassy slave driver. When my boss said *work*, I worked.

I explained the concept of self-motivation to Penelope on many occasions, along with the importance of having a Red Carpet Dream, but it never sunk in until I translated the concept into terms she could relate to. I told Penelope about an interview I'd seen with Cindy Crawford. When the reporter asked Cindy how she motivated herself, the savvy supermodel thought for a moment. "I may be Cindy Crawford, but even I work for Cindy Crawford!"

Penelope's eyes went wide. "So I should ask Cindy Crawford to be my boss?"

"Oh, Penelope." I shook my head. "No, Cindy Crawford cracks her own whip. And you ought to, too!"

The Strip-Down: You *can* achieve your Red Carpet Dream, but you'll fail if you put someone else in charge of your motivation, or if you decide to wait for the perfect circumstance or situation to happen before you begin.

Your Red Carpet Dream requires the proper mindset—the belief that you can do it—and consistent action. A weekend workshop or even a great book can point you in the right direction, but no one can take the steps except you. That's why you need to *crack your own whip*! I've consolidated this philosophy into an easy-to-remember equation:

Proper Mindset

+

Consistent Action

=

Red Carpet Dreams

Until you have the first half of the equation, you don't have squat. But when you crack that whip, I guarantee you'll move faster toward your Red Carpet Dream. So whip yourself as needed.

Stripper Tip #43: *Work Like the Rent Is Due*
Given that I started every night at the club in debt to the house fee, there was no time to screw around. I had to hook at least eight lap dances before I saw a profit. That was all the motivation I needed to hit the ground running and keep going!

So that meant I couldn't be like Bambi, who spent the first half of each night "warming up" by talking to regular lookie-loos who were never going to pony up the cash. Or like Trina, who spent so much time getting tarted up in the dressing room that by the time she hit the floor, the rush was already over. *Why bother, then?* I would think. I wasn't stripping for fun; I was stripping for money! If I wasn't *working like the rent was due*—and due tonight—then I was wasting my time.

Over the years, I came to realize that the line of demarcation between the women who survived the business and those who didn't was drawn in the way they approached their night. Women who took forever to get ready, women who opted to *hang out on the unemployment couch* (see

Stripper Tip #60), women who knew they were lollygagging with non-paying customers—all of them struggled to make rent, let alone turn a profit. But the women who aggressively worked the customers throughout their whole shifts saw it pay off in cold, hard cash!

The Strip-Down: Businesses that aren't hustling do not succeed. Tons of otherwise brilliant business babes who spend a lot of time hanging out on the Internet—telling everyone about how busy they are—in reality are not getting very much done at all.

If you *work like the rent is due*, you'll leave the office feeling proud of what you've accomplished, instead of overwhelmed by the progress you didn't make. When you put a high value on your time, you'll inherently gain a more proactive attitude toward generating income—after all, lost time equals lost business. You'll have time to play when your bills are paid and your Red Carpet Dream is moving in the right direction.

Stripper Tip #44: *Don't Light Your Own Cigarette*

One crickets-and-tumbleweeds night at the club, I slipped into a pleasant memory of a trip back home to Minnesota. My sister and I had arrived at my friend Frank's house for a long visit. It was a hot day, the car was full of luggage and I was exhausted from traveling.

As soon as we arrived, Frank and my sister started unloading my things, presumably thinking they were helping me out so I wouldn't be left carrying all my own bags. When

Frank reached the front door, he turned around to see how I was managing with my share. What he saw was me sauntering up to the front door without a thing in my arms except my handbag. As he and my sister exchanged a look of amazement, he laughed and said, "How did that just happen? How did she get us to carry her luggage?" I thanked them and then glided past them through the front door and went straight to the bar, where I made myself a cocktail. All that delegating had me pooped!

That inspired me to think about the tasks I could delegate at the club. The bouncers were already required to carry our workbags, and I couldn't delegate asking for dances or giving lap dances. As I lit up a cigarette, a brilliant idea occurred to me. What if I never had to light my own cigarette again? I'd never again scramble for matches or need to fill my lighter. Thus began a new experiment. It started with me slowly pulling out a cigarette, looking around the room with it dangling from my mouth and taking a deep, sexy breath. Without fail, a customer would approach within fifteen seconds, happy to help a damsel in distress, and offer to light it for me.

One dancer asked me how I always managed to get my cigarette lit so quickly. I responded, "It's because I believe I'm worth it. I believe that someone else wants to help me. And then I allow it to happen, every time." And here's what you can do. Start with a cigarette, master getting that lit and then move on to delegating other things in your life. Your time is valuable. And trust me, there's someone out there who would love to do what you don't want to do!

The Strip-Down: First: If you smoke, quit that habit, please! (I'm thirteen years clean, myself.) We're talking about metaphorical cigarettes, here. Second, if delegating to your assistant feels like a waste of time because you want the job done your way, I want you to consider that it's time to step back and re-prioritize. Red Carpet Dreams require enormous amounts of time and energy. You cannot do it all on your own. It's essential that you get the help you need, and frankly, my dear, you deserve it!

Handing over the reins can fill you with fear and anxiety, but delegating the small stuff will leave you with more face-to-face time for your clients, more time to strategize your next Red Carpet move and more opportunities to grow your company. As the face of your empire, you need to be on the town. Claim your domain kindly, share your chores to free up your time and *don't light your own cigarette.*

Stripper Tip #45: *Give It Your Least*
Many dancers wasted too much time in the dressing room prepping for their performances on the big stage. Rather than working the floor up until the very last minute, some would go so far as to redo their makeup and hair and put on whole new costumes as if they were dancing in the first run of a Vegas cabaret. Then, once onstage, they really went for the gold, frantically twirling and whirling and bumping and grinding like the fate of the world depended on it! At the conclusion of a six-minute performance, they would be so sweaty and exhausted that they would have to return to the dressing room to catch their breath, change their outfits and

redo their makeup and hair all over again.

These dancers put on quite a show, but they were failing to capitalize on the whole point of the stage dance, which is the brief celebrity status that you enjoy immediately afterwards. By the time they got back out to the floor to cash in on their performances, the fickle fancies of the customers had moved on to the next dancer. Wasn't making money the whole point?

I know that guys care a whole lot less about a girl's costume and dancing abilities than they do about her attitude. I tested this hypothesis one evening by doing my stage dance fully clothed. Instead of giving it my all, I simply worked the tip rail, lip-synched to the song, interacted with the customers and gave it my least. As soon as I hit the floor, I got dances. How easy! By considering what the customer really wanted (i.e. to watch a hot chick dance and have a good time with her afterwards), I made extra cash and saved time and energy in the process.

The Strip-Down: Your Red Carpet Dream needs momentum to keep it going. Save your most precious resources for things that have the most impact. Obsess over details when they count, but never let them slow you down. *Give it your least* and only spend significant time on significant things, like *asking for the dance* (see Stripper Tip #15).

Identify your momentum stealers. Are you obsessing over taglines, photos or website copy? Are you getting hung up on business cards? Grab a pen, and quickly jot down the first five items that come to mind. Go with your intuition. What does your gut tell you to stop ASAP? Don't over-think this; otherwise, you'll be back to putting on an elaborate stage show that's *not* making you money. Give your momentum stealers your least, so that you can give your money-makers your best.

Stripper Tip #46: *Level Up (And Let Them Adjust!)*
The summer I started dancing, I worked my required shifts and then some. I was eager to save money for school, and I welcomed all the experience (and cash) I could get. As the years passed, my enthusiasm for long shifts waned. Once I knew how to hustle like a pro, it was time to work smarter. I knew that I could make the same money, if not more, working shorter hours. Luckily, I had a reputation at the club for being as sharp as I was sassy, and I was prepared to use this to my advantage. My angle was simple: scare the pants off of management by insinuating legal implications.

I approached my manager and told him my "Suing for Profit" class (a totally fabricated name) had been moved to evening slots; therefore, I wouldn't be able to come in until 9:00 p.m. Considering the intimidating topic of my class and the reputation I'd created for myself—management's nickname for me was, no joke, the Militant Dancer—I knew he would rather succumb to my request than face the potential fury that a pissed off lawyer-in-training could deliver. And I was right. He shrugged his shoulders and said, "Okay. Just don't tell anyone else."

You would think my "Suing for Profit" class would have eventually ended (you know, like when the semester did), but it didn't. It went on throughout the rest of my time at the club. Since I was making the same amount of money for the club, management never mentioned it. They just adjusted to my leveling up!

The Strip-Down: Set your intentions for the long term. Work hard to pay your dues and establish your business foundation. And then, when you are good at what you do, level up. The better you get, the more you need to level up.

If you're good at what you do, people will accept the reality you offer them. So take a moment to think about where you need to upgrade. Can you raise your prices because you know that your quality and your turnaround time are so much better than most of what's out there? Narrow your products or services to only the ones that make you sing? Only book meetings on days that are convenient to your schedule? Brainstorm a bit, and you'll find something that's ready for an upgrade.

Warning: this may not be comfortable, but if you aren't continually pushing yourself out of your comfort zone, you're never going to grow your business. It's not easy to *level up (and let them adjust),* but it's absolutely essential for your progress! So revel in the fact that you're ahead of the curve. They'll catch up. And if they don't? They were never meant to keep up with you.

Stripper Tip #47: *Take a Break from Heelsville*
One of my all-time favorite club regulars was a young lad named James. James rarely had a five-dollar bill to his name and was utterly incapable of conversing about anything besides horror movies. If God had asked James to write a

brief thesis on the meaning of life, it would have been an exploration into the juxtaposed awesomeness of the Freddy and Jason slasher movies.

What made James special, in spite of his lack of social finesse or fiscal appeal, were his foot massages. He could talk Freddy to me all night in return for that kind of payola. Every night he was there, I made a point to get at least twenty minutes' worth of his divine touch.

Soon after submerging myself in the world of slasher flicks, I noticed that after my twenty minutes with James, I had more energy and a better mood for the rest of the night—which led, ultimately, to more money. Taking time off in the middle of my shift and getting out of my heels was like a twenty-minute trip out of Heelsville, and it really put the snap back in my thong. This epiphany gave me a new appreciation for the benefits of a mental and physical escape. In a job as physically intensive and mentally exhausting as stripping, a break was not a luxury—it was a necessity.

The Strip-Down: Giving yourself a short break in the workday will help you maintain a consistent, high-caliber level of performance. Working yourself to the bone isn't a sign of being a go-getter—it's a sign of idiocy! Remember, you're not doing this just for pleasure. You're doing this to amp your business. So give yourself luxurious permission to *take a break from Heelsville.*

Don't have a masseuse nearby for a quick foot rub? You can still take twenty minutes during your day to doodle, daydream, meditate, chitchat with someone who fills your energy pot or indulge in a tea party for one. Or better yet, if you work from home, get in your comfy bed for a twenty-minute catnap. Your empire requires you to feel refreshed every day, so don't be shy about adding a quick snooze to your action plan. You're not reinventing the wheel; you're creating a new mode of transportation—the Red Carpet Dream. After a twenty-minute quickie, you'll be ready to burn rubber!

Stripper Tip #48: *Know When to End the Dance*

If you recall, my very first Red Carpet Dream was to be a world-famous fashion designer—which, as it turns out, was one huge, unexpected lesson in patience. During my two years in the apparel design program, I spent most of my time ripping out seams—sleeves I had sewn in backwards, waistbands I had sewn in upside down, armholes I had sewn shut—instead of whipping out haute couture. Destroying the work I had created just to start over again was utterly soul-crushing.

When the tension and emotion reached particularly intense levels, it was always better for me to get up early the next morning and start fresh instead of straining my eyeballs until well after midnight. The fashion design industry is famous for quick and brutal burnouts, and I was determined not to fizzle before my time—or at least not before graduation.

I applied this same theory to my nights at the club. Sometimes I'd be on a moneymaking roll, and then, out of nowhere, nothing. Thanks to that lingering high-energy rush, it was nearly impossible to shift gears and sit around waiting for a customer to saunter through the door.

One evening, I was slammed for the first three hours

of my shift and made beaucoup bucks before the club suddenly emptied out. In the course of fifteen minutes, I went from making bank at a breakneck pace to chitchatting about Brad Pitt's behind with the other dancers. Titillating as it was, the serious lack of productivity was excruciating. I knew how nights like this played out, and I knew that even if a few more people did come through the door, I was better off leaving with my gains, enjoying a night at home and returning the next day with my mojo fully charged. I might've made a handful of grocery money if I'd stuck around, but getting a full night's sleep was worth so much more.

The Strip-Down: When something has stopped being useful, you can't keep trying to force it to life. And you can't be at your best if you're not fresh, focused or excited because you've been up all night, every night.

Energy, creativity and productivity have rhythms. Start paying attention to yours. Keep your eyes and ears open. Get intimately familiar with the ins and outs, the highs and lows of your business environment and how you fit in it. Never work from desperation. Adjust course as needed. Believe me when I say that you were born with intuition. Listen to it, and let it out to play. Trust it radically. It will save you time, money and mojo—and it will always let you *know when to end the dance.*

Stripper Tip #49: *Take a Chore Break*
Even I, the Queen of Hustle, had nights where I didn't want to work. But I still needed to *work like the rent was due* (see

Stripper Tip #43) because, frankly, it was. On nights like those, I knew what I had to do. I had to take a chore break.

Taking chore breaks was a practice I perfected in college. There were many times when I had gobs of homework and no interest in studying, especially for an algebra or biology test. Since dropping those classes wasn't an option, I developed a systematic zap of motivation. I turned off the TV and the phone (this was before I had a home computer), closed the blinds, shut my door and set my egg timer for ten minutes of hardcore, focused work.

Knowing that I only had to do my "chores" for ten minutes took the pressure off and gave me the space I needed to get in the mood. After the timer rang, I always gave myself permission to stop, but ninety percent of the time those ten minutes gave me the *oomph* I needed to keep going. I would ride the wave of self-propelled motivation until I finished my homework in one sitting. Afterwards, I would feel energized and proud of myself for taking care of business.

Back in the club, I used this same tactic whenever the urge to laze and daze hit. I didn't have my egg timer with me, so I improvised. I told myself that if I went around the club once and asked every single customer for a dance, then I could go back to the dressing room and resume being a lump. This, of course, rarely happened. Once I hit the floor, either a customer would buy a dance or I would quickly be inspired to get creative and dig into my bag of hustling tricks. Either way, all I ever needed was a bit of momentum to get the juices flowing, and then there was no looking back.

The Strip-Down: The next time you find yourself working on everything else but what you are really supposed to be working on, flash back to high school physics class. Remember the law of inertia? An object at rest tends to stay at rest, while an object in motion tends to stay in motion. This is the exact principle that comes into play when you *take a chore break*. It's all about shaking up your current mindset. Changing gears is difficult—especially when you have to do tasks that you don't enjoy—so create incentives you know will work. One way to fool yourself into a new momentum is to tell yourself that, after a short period of time, you can stop.

Determine what needs to be done and what you can do in a ten-minute block of time. Before you start working, give yourself clear boundaries and then *go*! Once the timer dings, you're done! By then, you'll be focused and committed to the new task at hand. So get the kitchen timer out, put *Scandal* on pause and take a ten-minute chore break to make phone calls, write web copy, pay bills or organize paperwork. Once you're done, you can get back to dinking around.

Stripper Tip #50: *It's Okay to Put On Your One-Inch Stilettos*
In the typical man's fantasy of strippers, women love to be naked, they orgasm every time they do a lap dance and they wear stilettos while running errands. Nothing would have made me happier than to live that fantasy—especially the part about wearing six-inch heels while pushing a shopping cart. (I've had an obsession with high heels ever since my first encounter with *Vogue*.) But by year eight of my career, my feet, knees and back were beginning to crack from the thousands of accumulated hours spent in high heels. My body hurt all the time—whether I was onstage, doing the

cat crawl or performing lap dances. But what could I do? I couldn't be a stripper without wearing stilettos. That was part of the mandatory business attire. Wasn't it?

The only time I'd seen the heel-free look was in the beginning of my career, when Little Darlin', a hippy nudist camp escapee, blessed us with barefoot performances that drew applause only for their comedic value. Still, Little Darlin' had managed to make money. In serious need of relief, I made a case for losing the giant heels.

Exhibit A: It was already a rule that dancers had to take off their shoes while giving lap dances to avoid damaging the couches. So why bother with six-inch heels when I was working the floor?

Exhibit B: 1 stood 6 feet 2 in platform stilettos. Alienating shorter, insecure men meant lost money.

Exhibit C: The club was so dark that unless I was at the bar getting a drink or dancing onstage, customers couldn't see my shoes anyway. And frankly—shoe fetishists aside—most customers couldn't care less about my footwear when I wasn't onstage.

Based on my conclusions, I decided to alternate between two pairs of stilettos—one gorgeous, ultra-sleek, sexy and glittery pair for my stage performances, and one utility pair for working the floor.

After my first shift working in my one-inch stilettos, I felt so good that the orgasm part of the aforementioned fantasy almost materialized. Not one customer noticed my orthopedics, and I didn't have to hear any remarks about my Amazonian height. Talk about making the right call!

The Strip-Down: Entrepreneurship is not a one-size-fits-all world. There are plenty of situations where your weaknesses will be challenged, which is why *it's okay to put on your one-inch stilettos*. Need a bunch of copy written for your site, but you would rather scrub the Mall of America with a toothbrush? Hire a writer. Know your words inside and out, but struggle with keeping track of your finances? Hire an accountant. Make it easy on yourself. Be honest about your strengths and weaknesses and act accordingly so you can focus on the areas where you're brilliant; that tiny shift might be the missing piece to world domination.

Stripper Tip #51: *Become a Mistress of Patience*

There are two types of strippers: those who rock the pole, and those who don't. I was the latter. I flat-out sucked. Back then, there were no pole-dancing classes for suburban moms or for budding strippers like myself, so I was on my own.

To add to my reluctance, I knew a dancer who had injured her neck falling from high up the pole. For two months, she had to wear a neck brace to work. She covered it in pink glitter, thinking it would look less orthopedic, but it didn't help. Her whole situation inspired me to keep my feet on the floor and to do everything in my power to avoid breaking a bone doing some fancy, spinny, flippy, twirly pole work.

But I knew I had to do *something* with the pole. I couldn't get up onstage and act like it wasn't there. I thought about just hanging from it, but upper body strength was not my forte. I didn't want to go to a gym and pump iron just so I could work a pole that didn't interest me in the first place.

Instead, I focused on what I did have in long, lean abundance: legs. I figured that if I could become flexible enough to do the splits on the pole, I would be able to wow the crowd in a way that no other dancer at the club could.

My initial hope was to have my new move ready to premiere in a month, but my long legs proved more stubborn than I had predicted. It took me an *entire year* to be able to do the splits. I would clean off my living room floor, turn the TV my way and commence the thirty-minute torturous stretching routine. But good things come to those who spread their legs. And waiting helps, too.

Even though it took me eleven months longer than I had originally planned, I never thought about giving up on what was to become my killer signature move. I knew there was a big payday waiting for me at the end of the pole, and sure enough, when I unveiled my splits, I received a standing ovation from my colleagues and spent the rest of the night collecting the payoff from men eager to see me do it again.

The Strip-Down: When he was a young lad, Justin Bieber used to sing and play his guitar on the streets of his hometown while all of his friends were probably playing video games. Imagine the stamina and determination that even a ridiculously adorable kid must have needed to stand out there on the street. He was talented, obviously, but more importantly, he was willing to put in the hard work, and that propelled him to the big stage.

So don't stop before the payoff! The hard truth about Red Carpet Dreams is that most people give up on them. Mastery takes time and practice. You need to be willing to invest both of those in your craft. What is something only you can do for your business that you *know* you need to work on? For me, that list included learning to write effectively, learning to coach and learning to speak in public. I've worked hard at these things for years. And they are finally paying off! So don't quit at the first sign of a roadblock. *Become a mistress of patience.* Put your head down and keep your stilettos moving, no matter how long it takes.

6. Be On Top!

WHINER OR WINNER?
WHAT'S IT GOING TO BE?

Stripper Tip #52: *Give Your Self-Confidence a Massage*
Working in an environment that is centered around being
naked, each dancer had her own wish list of surgical bodily
improvements for herself and the other dancers. After a
thorough dissection of each other's "flaws," what was once
a group of beautiful Cinderellas turned into a grotesque
gaggle of stepsisters whose only hope for normalcy and happiness could come through Dr. Prince Charming's scalpel.
My "flaws" included small ankles, long arms, flat rear, cellulite, thin lips, pale skin, small boobs and poorly shaped
eyebrows.

This constant exposure under such a ridiculous
microscope dictated that I either find a way to cope with my
"deformities" or shrivel up into a tiny, quivering mound of

self-loathing. Here's how I would reassure myself to avoid the latter situation:

1. Men fantasize about my cellulite.
2. This bikini on me makes Bo Derek look like a 4.
3. JLo's got nothing on this white girl's booty.
4. Perhaps I should wear ankle socks. I don't want to make the other women feel bad about their super-boring, uber-average ankles that look massive next to mine.
5. Victoria wants to use my ta-tas as her next big secret.
6. Monkey arms are a classic. They never go out of style.
7. Those poor ladies who aren't as ghostly pale as I am will need TONS of makeup if they ever want to dress up as Morticia Addams for Halloween.

While my "flaws" still existed in all their glory, by *giving my self-confidence a massage,* I was able to avoid paralysis and keep on with the show.

The Strip-Down: Chronic self-consciousness stopped being cool when high school ended. If you're going to hustle your business like you mean it, you need powerful self-confidence to take the bite out of criticism and an attitude that says you're sizzlin' hot. *Give your self-confidence a massage* so that all of your insecurities have no choice but to slink offstage forever!

Know what influences your energy. Poring over fashion magazines, tabloids and celebrity TV totally rocks when you need brain candy, but too much of it can leave you feeling ugly and drained. Focus your energy and your thoughts on what makes you feel good and sexy. *Give your self-confidence a massage,* and it will take a deep, satisfying sigh of relief.

Stripper Tip #53: *Be Aggressively Positive*

Remember my *Comrade of Kick-Ass*, Peggy (see Stripper Tip #20)? The one I thought was snobbish? Well, it turns out that what I had mistaken for arrogance was her best hustling secret.

Peggy was a positivist—and no, that's not a Seattle-based cult. Despite the fact that she'd been dancing for some time, Peggy was rarely critical about anything, while, unfortunately, I found myself complaining about everything: the club was stinky and smoky; there were no windows; the music was too loud; the customers were obnoxious; the managers were pushy; the work was exhausting; there were no benefits; my feet, knees and back hurt and on and on. But Peggy kept her lips buttoned, avoiding the drama. She was there to haul in cash, not complain.

Peggy made me realize that I'd grown into the thing I despised most: a big, fat whiner. I was embarrassed by how childish I must have sounded, complaining about a job that gave me decent cash and freedom. I admired Peggy's positivism and wanted to follow her example. So a few nights later, I drew a star on my hand with a black Sharpie and called it my "happy star"—even though it looked more like a crude prison tattoo. My happy star was going to keep me positive. I'd be like Peggy in no time.

The first time I needed my happy star was in the dressing room. I was already annoyed at Suzie Q, who was blabbering on about how her fake boobs—already super-plus porn size—needed to be bumped up a size or two. When I reached for my giant duffle bag, I gritted my teeth. After a night of hard work, my happy star had smeared—and had become sad and pathetic. Now I was complaining about Suzie Q *and* my messy little star. Not only was I failing at the positivist gig, but I'd become irony's joke in the process!

Leave it to Peggy, my aggressively positivist angel, to save the day. One look at the ruined star and she declared she had the perfect solution. The next day, she arrived to work with a beautifully wrapped box. Inside was a gorgeous rhinestone star attached to a silver chain. Short of getting a real tattoo, it was the perfect reminder to stay positive.

The Strip-Down: We're all guilty of complaining, but no one wants to be around someone who's constantly spewing negativity. Master the art of finding the silver lining in everything—a skill that translates into a happier, more productive, cash-producing day. If you're complaining about something that could be fixed, tweaked or overhauled, step up and fix it. If you're not prepared to act, keep your mouth zipped, *be aggressively positive* and discover the rewards of a drama-free work ethic.

Learning to focus on the positive is not a quick fix—it's a lifestyle change. So go easy on yourself. Pick one person, thing or situation that you chronically complain about, and make a commitment to not complain about that person, thing or situation for twenty-four hours. Declare your commitment on a piece of paper and give yourself a reminder—

wear your watch on the other wrist; pin a note on the inside of your dress; even draw your own happy star on your hand! (Tip: Carry a marker in your bag. Freshen your lip gloss; freshen your happy star!) Give yourself one assignment per day until your life and business are shining bright—complaint-free!

Stripper Tip #54: *Practice Radical Gratitude*
At the strip club, many men came to live out their fantasies of sex-symbol rock stardom. In their minds, the hot, bikini-clad babes were stalking their laps because they were the Kings of Effin' Mountain, not because the women wanted their money. Many of these guys had a hard time coming down from this ego-boosting experience back into reality, and this led to all sorts of rude behavior.

Hey, we were selling dances for cash. We didn't expect to be treated as if we were virgins bestowing our favors for free. But that is exactly why we all loved to shake it for Mr. Prim, as we called him. Mr. Prim, as in prim and proper, was a businessman who was borderline obsessive when it came to expressing gratitude. The words "Oh, thank you very much!" accounted for eighty percent of what came out of Mr. Prim's mouth. As the intensity of my dance increased, so did the intensity of his gratitude. It was oddly charming, very sweet and greatly appreciated.

There wasn't a woman in the club who didn't appreciate Mr. Prim's enthusiastic manners. We'd all make sure he had a good time, felt special and left the club happy, just like a real rock star!

The Strip-Down: I guarantee that Mr. Prim is still saying, "Oh, thank you very much!"—both in the strip club and out. You just can't fake that kind of radical gratitude. And if you remember to say thank you, your clients will want to do business with you. Practice radical gratitude with your colleagues, clients, friends and family, and you'll gain allies who will stand behind your Red Carpet Dream.

This is not about niceties or sending thank-you cards because that's what your mother always told you to do. This is about amplifying energy. Showing appreciation benefits everyone. Here are a few ways to say thank you and have fun at the same time:

1. Choose a book that you love, write a nice note on the inside cover and send a client an unexpected gift in the mail.

2. Buy a package of thank-you cards and write one card a week to a past, present or future client. Or go new school and send them a customized virtual thank-you card. Check out Red Stamp for their selection.

3. Go all out and join a corporate gift club like the CHOCbite Club. This way, you'll always have a full stock of unique, delicious sweet treats to give your clients.

You'll never run out of ways to *practice radical gratitude.* Say thank you enough and you may just inspire your clients and colleagues to send *you* thank-you cards.

Stripper Tip #55: *It's All Part of the Act*

Miriam was a petite dancer with massive dreadlocks. Although a few of the men might have appreciated her hairdo, she knew most customers wouldn't get it. To avoid wasting her hustle on answering questions about her hair, she wrapped her dreads on top of her head and donned a large red wig. Now, instead of looking like a Rasta chick, she looked like Ariel from Disney's *The Little Mermaid*—perfect fodder for a Disney fan's fantasy.

One evening, Little Miss Mermaid was onstage, swaying to Marvin Gaye's "Let's Get It On," and all eyes were on her as she effortlessly lunged into splits and bends that would cripple most dancers. As I watched her seductively slink and slither, I was equal parts proud and painfully jealous. My envy ended abruptly when, during one of her heel-to-head backbends, her stiletto caught her wig and ripped it off as she uncoiled. I braced myself for a horrible, awkward disaster, but Miriam grabbed the moment by the horns and, without a trace of visible concern, grabbed her wig, untangled it from her shoe and twirled it around like an accessory.

Then she elegantly approached the mirror, reapplied her giant red hair over her medicinal-looking nude wig cap, slyly looked to make sure everything was straight, put a big sexy smile on her face and continued with her routine. It was so smooth it could have been part of her act.

The Strip-Down: Nothing says more about your true grit than the way you recover from a clumsy stumble, a business boo-boo or a wardrobe malfunction. You can turn embarrassing situations to your advantage by rolling with the craziness. The next time you find yourself with your hair extensions falling out or a stiletto-clad foot in your mouth, recognize the opportunity to recover. Make a joke, do a dance, start to laugh, shake your booty—it doesn't matter, as long as you make it look like *it's all part of the act*.

And when someone else is responsible for a mishap, like misquoting your credentials or misinterpreting your company, take a deep breath and then exhale. Assume that it was an innocent mistake; turning it into a diva moment will not help your reputation. Remember all the mistakes you've made in the past, and move on. Once you've corrected the mishap, you can transition into the important part of the conversation: hustling your product or service.

Stripper Tip #56: *Tune Them Out, Tune You In*

One night, as I was making my rounds, I politely asked a customer if he wanted a dance.

"No!" he replied. "You're ugly!" Now, I had encountered plenty of cruel customers who said I was too tall; my boobies weren't big enough; my rear was too flat; my hair wasn't blonde enough, dark enough or red enough and on and on, but *never* had someone insulted me with a word like *ugly*. My knee-jerk reaction was to slap him across the face. So I did.

The manager found me in the dressing room, where I'd retreated in shock, and asked if I had slapped a customer. I had no choice but to tell the truth. And then he informed me that my customer was calling the cops to report an assault. ACK!

When the police arrived, I was brought into the

manager's office for questioning. I started off by explaining exactly what the customer had said to me, and before I could even finish, the cop said, "I've heard enough. That guy is a total jerk! Sorry for wasting your time." Whew! Close call. Still, I knew I had to get my anger under control before someone else dared to use that word with me again.

From that point on, whenever someone said something rude to me, I pretended that I had a special translator in my ear that turned his negative comment into a positive one. For example, I would ask someone in the club for a dance and, after getting the creepy once-over and a "No, thanks," my supersonic ear translator would read it as "Oh, my God, you are so gorgeous. I would give anything to have a dance from you, but I'm afraid of what my friends will say. You see, I'm a stupid jerk, and by law I'm only allowed to get dances from silicone-stuffed Barbie dolls."

This special translation made me feel better about myself and about the idiot who had just insulted me. *Tuning them out and tuning me in* helped give me that swagger that comes from not giving a hot damn about what other people think.

The Strip-Down: It's a fact of life: Some people are just jerks. And some jerks get really stirred up when they see someone following her dreams, living boldly and taking the kinds of chances that they themselves have never had the courage to take. But knowing that doesn't always take the sting out of interacting with them! So make it easier on yourself, and have a little fun at the same time. Translate whatever guff the mindless naysayers are spouting into something silly and cartoony that also happens to include one (or several!) big important truths about you and your business. Here, try a few on for size:

- "We are so intimidated by your incredible work and your stunning beauty that we cannot possibly work with you."
- "I am having a hard time accepting the fact that a gorgeous queen like yourself would ever want to waste time on a lowly serf like me, so instead I am saying whatever crazy thing pops into my head."
- "Oops! I am so nervous around you that I am being a complete loser to protect my sensitive, eggshell-like feelings! I hope to grow up soon!"

It works, I promise. And once you *tune them out,* you'll realize how easy it is to *tune you in.*

Stripper Tip #57: *Nice Girls Say No*

At the strip club, I often felt like a broken record, and the only song on the album was "No!" *No, you can't touch me. No, you can't kiss me. No, I won't go home with you. No, I won't go on a date with you. No, I won't pretend to be your girlfriend so you can make your ex-girlfriend jealous.* Saying no to customers at the club was easy. Saying no in my own life was a little more complicated.

I was a nice person! Nice people didn't say no to the people they cared about! So when I was asked to hang out, do this, do that, go here, go there—and yes, even loan money—I would always say yes, even when I had other priorities, like school. Never mind that because my job and school requirements were so strenuous, I needed most of my personal time to take care of, well, me. Besides which, I really enjoyed my solitude. Reading, decorating my apartment and designing new outfits were all activities that kept me centered and refreshed. My "me time" wasn't a luxury, it was a necessity.

So, tired of being mean to myself—allowing time sucks and energy vampires into my life—I decided to be nice to myself and start saying no, just like in the club. The first casualty was a friend of mine who seemed to relocate every six months. My friend knew she could rely on me for moving muscle, but the amount of time and energy I had spent on her previous moves, coupled with the fact that she could afford to hire professional help, left me with no choice but to explain that the free labor she had come to rely on was no longer available. It wasn't easy to disappoint a friend; however, I'm a nice girl, so I said no . . . nicely.

The Strip-Down: Nice girls say no, so quit being naughty. It's actually mean to say yes to something that you don't really want to do. Being on committees you don't care about will slow down others who do care. You waste other people's time when you meet with them and you know you won't be doing business with them. Saying yes when your heart's not in it creates resentment in *your* heart, which takes up precious space and might ultimately make you cranky and bitter. Ew! Why let that happen? When you're nice *to yourself* and say no, you'll have more time to be on committees that you do care about. You'll know who you want to do business with and you just might even want to help your friends out more!

Take a look at your calendar and make a list of all the activities you've participated in over the last month. Divide them into two columns: professional and personal. Once you've written down every last book club, community meeting, coffee date and trip to the gym, take out a marker and highlight the five activities in each column that you enjoyed the most. Then, take another look and cross out the five activities you enjoyed the least. How many of your favorite activities line up with your Red Carpet Dream? How many of the activities you crossed out do? If you're doing things you don't enjoy AND they don't bring you closer to your Red Carpet Dream, why are you wasting your time? Use this exercise to reassess your plans and commitments for the next month. You don't have to participate in everything just because it lands in your inbox, especially if you'd rather have time to salsa dance with your Red Carpet Dream.

Stripper Tip #58: *Refuse to Be Bullied*

One particularly long night, I was famished and ready to eat. My favorite foot-long turkey-and-Swiss sandwich was waiting in the dressing room fridge. But when I opened the fridge, there was no sandwich. After frantically searching the locker room, I spotted a crumpled Subway wrapper shoved into the back of a top shelf. *Nico!*

To be fair, I had been warned about Nico—the club's resident heroin addict—whose favorite pastimes included nodding off into a comatose state and eating other dancers' food. But I hadn't taken the warning seriously, and it seemed my luck had run out. I was not going to put up with someone eating my food. You could use my hairspray, makeup or perfume, and even borrow an outfit, but I drew the line when it came to my turkey with extra mayo. I promptly removed the remaining one-third of my sandwich from the crumpled wrapper, located Nico's leather motorcycle jacket on the coat rack, unzipped the front left pocket, and squished the remaining bread, turkey, cheese, mustard, mayo, vinegar, oil, salt, pepper, lettuce and tomato into every crack and seam. If Nico wanted my sandwich, she could have it to go. She never touched my sandwiches again.

The Strip-Down: I really hope you don't work around anyone who needs a sandwich squished into her jacket, and in any case, physical or violent reactions are never appropriate. I had a client whose boss tossed her stinky lunch leftovers into the garbage can underneath my client's desk every day. My client couldn't exactly retaliate stripper-style, but she had to put the kibosh on the stench. Taking inspiration from my own experience, she donned her refuse-to-be-bullied stilettos and had a frank, professional conversation with her boss. The boss apologized and admitted that she hadn't even considered the resentment her stinky lunch might cause. It never happened again, and now that client is running her own business. You can rest assured she will never dispose of her unfinished sandwich beneath an employee's desk.

If your boundaries aren't clearly drawn, what's going to stop someone from walking all over you, especially when you're working together for the first time? When someone flagrantly crosses the line, take action immediately. Respectfully and gracefully communicate clearly that you *refuse to be bullied*.

Stripper Tip #59: *B-Slap Your Obstacles Down*

In my time on the pole, each club had its own culture and code of ethics. There was always an established system of unwritten rules that new dancers had to learn quickly if they wanted to survive. A perfect example was club territory. Aggressive dancers who had been at the club a long time would stake their claims on certain customers. Other dancers might get a shot, but the "proprietor" had the right of first refusal. New dancers who ignored this nuance paid with a nasty smackdown in the dressing room.

One evening, a new girl made the mistake of dancing for a customer who'd been claimed by Bridgette, who stood six feet tall and sported a platinum wig. We all knew what was coming, and we figured there'd be blood.

Outside the dressing room, the other nosy dancers and I could hear the anger in Bridgette's voice. We heard the sound of fist hitting flesh, a *Pop!* so loud that it made us jump. The door opened and out strolled the newbie. She walked right by us like nothing had happened and headed straight for Bridgette's customer. Inside, sobbing on the floor, with her wig lying next to her and blood pouring from her nose, was Bridgette. She had been b-slapped six ways to Sunday.

The newbie had a choice. She could take a beating or administer one. By standing up for herself, she moved right to the top of the pole and earned more money. After that night, she was a newbie no more. She didn't go looking for a fight, but when the fight found her, she didn't back down, and she won.

The Strip-Down: As long as you're breathing, you'll be facing down obstacles. Problems are a huge part of life, so getting better at dealing with them is a smart thing to do. And, sometimes, your best strategy is to stand up, step up and *b-slap your obstacles down*! Maybe your b-slap is to refuse to listen to your own negative self-talk, or to finally get an ugly argument sorted out so that you can put an end to the constant, low-level worry around it. Go head-to-head, face-to-face, eyeball-to-eyeball with each problem.

In fact, do it right now. Grab a pen and jot down your top three obstacles. Next, write down one thing you can do, right this second, to lay the smack down on each one. Hint: This is where you unleash your inner bitch. She's got important things to say to you, and maybe to the world! C'mon, you know she's in there. Let her out, let her speak, let her be heard. Take notes. And then act on them!

7. Don't Be That Girl!

SERIOUSLY—AVOID THESE SCENARIOS.
THEY'RE WORSE THAN A FAKE
DESIGNER HANDBAG.

Stripper Tip #60: *Avoid the Unemployment Couch*
No matter where I worked, the club always had an unemployment couch. This was where the dancers who weren't busy
with customers hung out. I spent many hours on the unemployment couch in my early days, hemming and hawing
with my "unemployed" comrades. Cigarette after cigarette,
I created artificial bonds with these women by exchanging
negative, mean-spirited comments about customers and
other dancers.

   "Oh my God, look at Jasmine! Does she ever change
her facial expression?" Or, "I can't believe Toni still dances
like it's her first day." Or, "Hey, is that a Maine lobster or
Gigi? Geez, she really needs to stay out of that tanning bed!"
Or, "Don't talk to the dude in the back row—I think he's

drunk on cough syrup."

We had some great laughs, but most of my time spent on the unemployment couch was a colossal waste of energy. Nothing was more depressing than hanging out with anxious, mean-spirited, idle dancers, especially when I felt equally anxious, mean-spirited and idle. We spiraled down together.

One night, when the evening lull hit and the unemployment couch had opened for business, I decided to use that dead time to do something positive and productive. I called an old friend and we had a meaningful conversation about boys and lip gloss. The next night, I organized my locker so neatly that the Container Store would have wanted to put it on display. And the next night I sat by myself and meditated the best I could with pumpin' rave music blasting in the club. After three nights of avoiding the unemployment couch, my stress level was down and my mood was up. And whenever my mood was up, my income went up. Booyah!

The Strip-Down: Whether you are gainfully employed, underemployed or unemployed, *avoid the unemployment couch*. Negativity feeds on negativity and gives birth to pessimism. There's no need to make a glum situation worse. Make a bold move and avoid negative people, conversations and media.

Instead, use your downtime to do things that make you happy. Listen to inspiring music, meditate and practice yoga, drink tea. Read books that amp your energy and light a match under your optimism, like Wayne Dyer's *Wishes Fulfilled* and Eckhart Tolle's *A New Earth*.

Any time you start to feel yourself being drawn to

the unemployment couch, redirect that misery, flip the TV channel and sit on the happy couch instead. It is your choice as to which couch to sit on. Will it be the life-sucks couch or the life-is-awesome couch?

Stripper Tip #61: *Don't Let the Throw Rug Distract You*
Helen and I met during a college biology class. One afternoon, while sifting through frog guts and trying not to gag from the smell of formaldehyde, she and I discovered we were both strippers with drive and Red Carpet Dreams. She wanted to be a doctor and I, at that point, had shifted my Red Carpet Dream from world-famous fashion designer to women's rights lawyer. Helen and I became fast friends.

Unfortunately for me, Helen transferred to a private college the following semester. When we finally met for coffee one day, I sadly discovered that she no longer wanted to be a doctor and would be dropping out of school mid-semester to work the Vegas strip until she figured out what to do with her life.

Helen's abrupt change of plans was disappointing and worrisome. I told her to at least finish the semester, see a career counselor and not give up. I certainly could relate to changing Red Carpet Dreams and how confusing that could be. She assured me that this was only a temporary gig, and that she would return to her studies in a few months when she was more focused.

Six months later, I heard that Helen had moved to Vegas permanently. Instead of returning to school, she was going to keep working the strip and saving money and *then* figure out what she wanted to do. I happen to know that Helen never became a doctor. She never even got close. Another smart, capable woman's Red Carpet Dream had been sacked by a throw rug.

The Strip-Down: Throw rugs are the bright, shiny temptations that draw your eyes away from your Red Carpet Dream. Sometimes a throw rug can be money—lots of money—but a paycheck in itself is not a Red Carpet Dream. Throw rugs are conveniently placed near major obstacles, mental roadblocks and overwhelming fears. You'll find them hiding, often in the form of excuses, whenever you doubt yourself and need an easier option. Their lure is instant gratification, convenience and comfort. When the glam eventually fades and grand opportunities have moved on, you'll realize that these throw rugs lead nowhere.

To ward off the temptation of throw rugs, consider the following questions:

- Are the activities, opportunities and people in your life going to propel you towards your Red Carpet Dream, or prevent you from following through?
- Are the activities, opportunities and people in your life going to connect you to the people, places and things you need to achieve your Red Carpet Dream?

Ask yourself these questions every day for thirty days. If you consistently decide that you have been blinded by instant gratification, convenience and comfort, toss that throw rug aside. *Don't let the throw rug distract you!* Hold tight to your thick, plush, luxurious red carpet and don't let go!

Stripper Tip #62: *Never Gossip About Your Competition*
I was standing at the bar one evening waiting for a soda, when another dancer walked up to me. "I would avoid the dressing room tonight," she said. "Mercedes just told everyone that she's going to beat the crap out of you for calling her a bad dancer."

Oh, no, I thought. *Open mouth and insert stiletto*. I was new to the club and the last thing I needed was trouble. I spent the rest of that night avoiding the dressing room and regretting my indiscretions. I managed to make it through the night without incident, but Mercedes' wrath never waned. Although she never physically accosted me, she continued issuing threats and insults for months via her posse. I spent much of those months on edge, anticipating an ugly confrontation.

That one stupid conversation I had in which I called Mercedes a bad dancer cost me hundreds of hours of stress and worry. My relief finally came when Mercedes left the club. The drama and the ugliness had drained my energy and screwed with my head. Turns out, harmony was important to me in the workplace. I decided to keep my lips shut at all times.

The Strip-Down: Gossiping about your competition is not a good idea. Sure, it can be juicy fun, but the risk-to-reward ratio is dangerously high. One trite little gossip session can easily turn into a professional nightmare. The person you slam today might be the person doing business with you tomorrow.

Even if you're hanging with a group of business friends who are participating in a game of gossip, don't succumb to peer pressure. *Never gossip about your competition.* You never know when karmic repercussions will arrive at the party in the form of someone working with—or for—that very person you're gossiping about.

Make it easier on yourself by always assuming that workplace gossip will eventually bite you squarely in the moneymaker. Choosing not to gossip gives you one hundred percent control of the outcome and keeps your opportunities open. So seal those lips, baby.

Stripper Tip #63: *Don't Forget Where You Came From*

Like many women new to the club scene, Serengeti was full of rookie vigor. But unlike a lot of other newbies, she was also humble. Her unrelenting enthusiasm may have made her a tad annoying, but her I-want-to-learn-everything attitude made it easy to like her. She had a way of asking for advice that triggered a maternal response in even the grouchiest of dancers. Soon, we were all rooting for her to make it. And make it she did, the lovable scamp! With the collective support of the other dancers, Serengeti became a perennial top earner at the club.

That's when our "little sis" became a big pain in the ass.

Two months after hitting the big time, the scrappy kid you couldn't help but love had completely morphed into a full-on nightmare. Instead of positive energy, Serengeti was radiating arrogance and attitude. She sauntered through the club as though it were hers and looked upon the other dancers as mere annoyances that someone of her caliber shouldn't have to deal with. For the rest of us, this ego trip became a slap in our collective face.

I only need one finger to count the number of times throughout my whole career that a group of strippers came together in the name of a single cause. Every girl had reached her tipping point with this chick's ego, and through a back-room intervention campaign we hatched Operation Sayonara, a simple yet diabolical plan that we knew would work. The plan consisted solely of us aggressively, systematically and enthusiastically ignoring Serengeti.

And oh, did it work. After only the second day of Operation Sayonara, Serengeti got the message and fled the club in tears. It was sad that our one-time protégé had forced us into taking such severe actions. But when you bite the hands that lifted you up, you should expect those hands to drop you, and fast.

The Strip-Down: Success is not an accident. Lots of people have helped boost you to superstardom. Losing your connection with reality will alienate the very people on whom you depend. Things change quickly—and trust me, if you're mistreating people today, they will be the ones you need most tomorrow. Make it a daily habit to honor the other stars that share your galaxy.

A healthy sense of self-confidence is vital to success, but *don't forget where you came from.* If you feel your head growing bigger with success, consider it a smart business decision to shrink that thing before your ego explodes. Not sure if this applies to you? Ask those who've helped you the most if your ego has overtaken the rest of your personality. They'll be only too happy to let you know exactly what they think.

Stripper Tip #64: *Never Complain in the Company of Customers*

At the club, when customers asked me how business was going, I always gave the same reply: "Great, really great!" The last thing I wanted to do was come across as unsuccessful or desperate.

I learned this lesson after a customer told me about a dancer who had launched into a rant about how much she hated her job, the club and the other dancers. The guy was there to escape the pressures of his own job as a salesman, and the last thing he wanted to hear was how much her job sucked. He had arrived at the club ready to pay for rock-star treatment. Talk about an instant turnoff. If he had wanted to listen to some malcontent moan about the sorrows of life, he could have had a conversation with himself for free.

As a stripper, I was a service-providing professional, period. No one cared how I was *really* doing—they wanted to be entertained! From that point on, I never complained in front of a customer. At times, it was difficult to restrain myself from venting to a seemingly willing victim, but at least I know no one ever walked away from me thinking, "Well, I wanted to buy a dance from her until . . ."

The Strip-Down: Complaining is a huge turnoff. One whiff and your customers will run away. Fast. No matter how good your product or service is. Customers want to know that their money is in good hands. They do not want to know about any issues behind the scenes. It's your job to wrap your products and services with a bow of one hundred percent confidence. No one needs to know about your problems unless you're telling someone who is part of your company or in your inner sanctum of trust and support. It's *your* job to figure out your company's challenges—NOT your customers' job. Do not air your dirty laundry to your clients. They don't care. They don't want to know about it. And they definitely don't want to hear about it. And remember, complaining on social media is still *complaining in the company of customers—don't do it*. Trust me, your clients and your potential clients are watching you.

Stripper Tip #65: *Don't Strip Off the Clock*

Blame it on grunge rock or strong espresso, but back in the '90s, Seattle was a national hub for sex, drugs and rock 'n' roll. The town was alive with debauchery, and the wild child in me took to that scene. The parties I frequented were rife with all the cliché elements you might expect, but the one thing I didn't like was the expectation that I would act like a stripper outside the club.

At work, indulging someone's fantasy was my *job*. Period. Outside of work, I was college-bound, book-loving Erika. I was *not* a topless exhibition waiting to happen and I was *not* pleased when strange men at a party would ask me for a dance. I've never been to any party where a lawyer would write up a legal brief as a courtesy or a doctor would give you a physical at no charge, so why would you expect to see a stripper dancing for free?

I didn't work outside of work. At all. I'd seen, close-up, what had happened to my friend Gigi. She'd started "working" at parties and became a lap-dance party favor—and things went south for her very quickly! I knew that stripping off the clock would blur the line between my job and my private behavior, which would cheapen me, and that would affect my sense of self-worth—which would then affect my ability to make money at the club. And I don't need to remind you that I was there to make money!

The Strip-Down: If you're not being vigilant about getting paid for your work, you could find yourself running out of steam. It's bad for your bank account, for your schedule and for expectations (both yours and your clientele's).

If you have expertise, you need to get paid for it. Period! I recommend that you dole out freebies (see Stripper Tip #24: *Free Samples Get 'Em in the Door*), but always do it on your terms, and during work hours. Maintain clear boundaries between your work time and your free time. Inform whoever asks that you *don't strip off the clock* and they can pay for your services during working hours. Hand them your business card and *ask for the dance* (see Stripper Tip #15). Oftentimes, you can close a deal on the spot instead of working for free. If you are confident in your abilities and they want what you are selling, your customers will not have a problem paying for your work.

Stripper Tip #66: *Don't Dance for Difficult People*

It didn't matter if my strip club customers were movie stars, TV stars, rock stars, ex-cons, thugs, gangsters, professors, filmmakers, professional athletes, over-eighteen high school jocks, Ivy League PhD candidates, retired bankers, attorneys, fishermen, tourists, engineers, bored married couples, off-duty cops or out-of-town business executives; what did matter was that, honestly, most of them were decent people.

It took a lot for me to say "Your money's no good" to a certain type of customer, but I learned to do it early in my career, after an encounter with four out-of-town businessmen. Shortly after sitting down with them for a drink, I secretly dubbed them Jerk #1, Jerk #2, Jerk #3 and Jerk #4. I was momentarily delighted when Jerk #4 opened up his wallet and produced a crisp hundred-dollar bill. However, he proceeded to rip Mr. Franklin in two, handing me one half and keeping the other.

"Sleep with me and I'll give you the other half," he teased. Smiling, I took my part of the hundred and tossed it into the burning candle resting on their table. While my half of the Benjamin burned, I replied with a simple "No, thank you," and walked away.

My self-respect was worth more than the temporary financial loss. That night I felt so proud about what I had done that my stripper mojo was ablaze. I was in control, my momentum was unstoppable and I walked out with a pile of cash.

The Strip-Down: Difficult people are everywhere, and you don't need to work with them to be successful. They may be good for quick cash, and refusing money is hard—but doing business with jerks is harder. You will soon understand the law of diminishing returns as their bullshit and drama steal your time, energy and positivity. So create a weasel-free zone and you'll be rewarded with clients who appreciate and respect you.

Here's how it works. If someone's a jerk, don't work with them, don't partner with them, don't sit next to them, don't look at them, don't speak to them and don't give them an ounce of your time or energy. If you find you're already doing business with a creep, take control. End the relationship as swiftly as possible, and in the future, *don't dance for difficult people!*

Stripper Tip #67: *Jealousy Kills—It Doesn't Pay the Bills!* You can't get promoted at a strip club. For all of us, every night, the fight for cash supremacy started from scratch, with no guarantee any of us would bring home anything to show for our work.

The only measure of success in the club was making loads of cash, and that brought out the worst in every dancer. Bragging became a sport, especially for Jenna, the club's top moneymaker. She had brains, the body of a Playmate of the Year—and a propensity for rubbing her cash in our faces. While the rest of us were in the dressing room counting twenties and fifties, Jenna was counting her toppling pile of hundred-dollar bills.

What killed me more than watching Jenna count her stash was hearing another dancer, Alexandra, tell her, "Good for you! That's fantastic!" After weeks of observing her congratulatory spirit, I asked Alexandra what the deal was with her bouncy cheerleader attitude. She explained that, in the past, she couldn't sleep at night because she was so jealous of Jenna's income. Then, after having a nightmare in which she was Jenna's cash-counting employee, she had a breakthrough. What if she stopped caring how much money Jenna was making? What if she was happy for her instead?

Alexandra decided she would give this new mentality a trial period. At the end of two weeks, if she wasn't feeling better, she could go back to jealous insomnia. But the trial worked! Choosing to be happy instead of bitter, Alexandra no longer felt jealous. With more oomph and joy to work the hustle, soon she was making more money than ever.

The Strip-Down: If you're busy watching Jenna Millionaire wave her hundreds at the party, that's what you're doing: watching. You're watching someone else do the networking, shaking hands with potential clients, enjoying the free Champagne. Talk about a masochistic energy drain.

Take a step back and observe what she's doing right. Watch her business moves. Discover who she is hanging out with, who she does business with. How did she get where she is? Even better, ask her to lunch—your treat—and uncover how she's working her "dance." You might find you can replicate her success with similar moves. Or it might turn out that upon closer inspection, her life is no better than yours. The sooner you learn that *jealousy kills—it doesn't pay the bills*, the faster you can make your own Red Carpet Dream a reality. Go over and shake her hand with a genuine smile. You never know—next year, she might be dancing with you!

Stripper Tip #68: *You Are a Princess. Take Charge.*
Waiting in a long line to use the restroom, I knew the time for tolerance was over. The club's public restrooms had been padlocked recently, and all the dancers were reduced to sharing a bathroom (with no stall) adjacent to the dressing room.

Picture five women waiting to pee, squeezed together in a tiny dressing room while other dancers were milling around getting dressed. Then imagine what happened when the non-commercial toilet—not meant to handle a hundred flushes a night—broke. I never imagined, back when I was a kid and my dad was teaching me rudimentary plumbing skills, that I would one day be distinguished as The Only Stripper Who Could Fix the Toilet.

Approaching club management with any grievance was always a dicey proposition. It's not like we had a union steward. Complaining usually got you nowhere, or worse, brought some kind of punishment, like a bad shift. But this toilet had reached its literal breaking point.

Two nights after the plumbing emergency, I was the top earner. I figured it was the best possible time to bring up the toilet situation. My manager not only listened attentively to what I had to say, but he actually agreed with me. Victory! Within days, the public restroom was opened back up and I could finally pee in peace.

The Strip-Down: What are you tolerating that a princess like you shouldn't have to put up with? Maybe you're letting clients get away with not paying you on time. Or putting up with a roof leak because you don't want to call the landlord. Or maybe the problem is something to do with you—like hating to organize your files. Whatever it is, let the princess in you banish the offender from your kingdom. Off with its head!

And when the princess is done, come up with five essential "I Will Not Tolerate" rules, such as:

- I will not tolerate customers not paying on time.
- I will not tolerate poor working conditions.
- I will not tolerate disorganized files.
- I will not tolerate customers who miss deadlines.
- I will not tolerate lame networking events.

In other words, *princess, take charge.*

Your Next Dance Moves

Now, I know you did *all* the exercises and answered *all* the questions in the Strip-Downs, but I don't want *Think Like a Stripper* to be just another business book that you read and then put on your shelf (or forget about on your iPad). I'm living proof—and so are my clients—that if you think like a stripper, you will be successful.

We may have reached the end of the book, but we are not done. Here are a few more things you can do to up your confidence, attract more clients and rule your market.

#1. Ask yourself which Stripper Tip scares you the most and take baby steps until the action comes naturally.

#2. Choose three of your favorite Stripper Tips each month and make a commitment to master them.

#3. Memorize the Strip-O-Pedia (page 131) and add more definitions of your own to the list.

I'd also love to be a part of your Red Carpet Dream!

Visit me online at www.DailyWhip.com
and sign up for FREE tips on how to whip
your business into shape.

Tweet me @dailywhip and tell me your favorite
Stripper Tip, tagging it with #ThinkLikeAStripper.

Hang out with me at Facebook.com/DailyWhip for
more tips, tricks and tools to up your confidence,
attract more clients and rule your market.

Strip-O-Pedia

A GLOSSARY OF SOME OF THE
TERMS USED IN THIS BOOK.
APPLY THEM JUDICIOUSLY!

Asking for the Dance: The big, fearless step of asking your customer to buy your product or service.

Bringing Your B-Cup Game: Showing up as *you*, regardless of what the norm is, and being a creative bootstrapper so that your business will succeed.

Business Seductress Style: That thing that defines your "you-ness" and makes your customers want to throw money at you.

Comrade of Kick-Ass: A peer whose business goals are similar to yours, and on whom you can count to have your back so that you can improve your skills and cash situation.

Double-Ds: A strategic partnership/joint venture you enter into for mutual business benefit.

Giving It Your Least: Identifying the parts of your business you can outsource or do away with, so that you can focus your genius on your big moneymakers.

Red Carpet Dream: The dream that ties your entire life up into a pretty bow. The one that terrifies you, because you know you're meant to achieve it.

Removing the Safety Net: The moment you let go of your backup plans and fully commit to your Red Carpet Dream.

Taking a Chore Break: Setting a short period of time for buckling down and doing whatever you're procrastinating on. When the time's up, you'll be free to go—but you probably won't want to.

Throw Rug: The smaller, disposable version of your Red Carpet Dream, which is incredibly easy to stumble over. To be avoided at all costs.

Tuning Them Out, Tuning You In: Deflecting haters and naysayers by only listening to the truth about yourself and what it is you're doing.

Two Bikinis: The essential marketing needed to bring in the sale. No bells or whistles required.

Radical Gratitude

A team of people helped me concept, write and complete this book over the past four years, and another team helped me launch it. Words do not even begin to capture my radical gratitude, but here's my sincerest attempt.

Thank you to:

My husband. For your love and support, and for always listening, even if you've heard it a thousand times before—and you probably have. I'm the luckiest girl in the world to share my life with you.

My dad. For teaching me that success in business requires extreme persistence, patience and creativity.

My mom. For teaching me that success in life requires love and forgiveness.

Chad Haverfield. Jolene Brink. Melissa DeLay. Emma Alvarez Gibson. For contributing words, ideas and editorial feedback, and for being a pillar in my creative process.

Sonja Trejo. For showing me that when I'm having fun my writing voice comes out to play.

Deborah Patricelli Brandt. For inspiring brainstorming energy on high.

Ruth Ann Harnisch. For being my punk rock fairy godmother, for encouraging me on the long march to be my best and for not going easy on me.

Mark Levine. For providing a spot-on title and planting the seed for the book.

Kate Ankofski. Katie Mehas. For your keen editing and opinions.

Hillcrest Media. For your incredible customer service and brilliant book design.

Elizabeth Marshall. Victoria Prozan. Srinivas Rao. Jamie DuBose. Janica Smith. Helen Hunter Mackenzie. For being a kick-ass book launch team.

Daily WhipSTARS. For sharing your hearts and your Red Carpet Dreams with me. I am deeply honored to whip your businesses into shape.

About the Author

Erika Lyremark, the creator and mastermind behind Daily Whip, is a green smoothie-drinking, yoga-loving, bossypants-wearing ex-stripper who lives to help other women entrepreneurs make their Red Carpet Dreams a reality.

Originally from Minneapolis, she spent nearly a decade "on the pole" in Seattle before moving back home to build a commercial real estate company with her father and start Daily Whip.

Married to the sweetest, smartest and sexiest man in the world, Erika continues to make her home in Minneapolis, to the surprise of nearly everyone.